Practical Strategies for Meeting the Rigorous *Common Core State Standards* for Reading
(Grades K-2):
A Teacher Handbook – Professional Development Series

By

Denise Gudwin, PhD

© Denise M. Gudwin www.denise.gudwin.org

All material in this book not specifically identified as being reprinted from another source is copyright © 2013 by Denise M. Gudwin, Ph.D. Permission is granted to make copies for your individual classroom use only. Reproduction of these materials for an entire school or district is prohibited, without the prior written consent of the author. You may not distribute, copy, or otherwise reproduce any of this book for sale or for commercial use without written permission from the author.

Denise M. Gudwin, Ph.D.
Seattle, WA

denisegudwinconsulting@gmail.com

Check out my WEBSITE at www.denise.gudwin.org
for additional resources and information.

About Your Instructor

DR. DENISE GUDWIN is an acclaimed teacher and outstanding nationally recognized presenter and school-site consultant in the areas of literacy, learning disabilities, mentoring/coaching, differentiated instruction, inclusive /co-teaching practices, and Response to Intervention. Experienced as a classroom teacher, curriculum specialist, staff developer, central office administrator, and university instructor, Denise brings 35 years of experience working with students who have reading difficulties. Thirty of those years include twenty years in the classroom, and ten years in the central office as an instructional supervisor for Programs for Learning Disabilities, and as an executive director for Professional Development.

Denise is the author of PRACTICAL STRATEGIES FOR MEETING THE RIGOROUS COMMON CORE STATE STANDARDS FOR READING (GRADES K-2), the extensive resource handbook each participant will receive at the seminar. Denise is co-author of a book about mentoring new teachers by Corwin titled, Mentoring and Coaching: A Lifeline for Teachers in Culturally and Linguistically Diverse Classroom (2010); Phonological Awareness and Early Literacy Assessment (Wright Group); Professional Development: Assisting Urban Schools in Making Annual Yearly Progress, in the Journal of Urban Learning, Teaching, and Research (Volume 3, September 2007); and A Qualitative Study of New/Early Career Special Education Teacher Retention in a Multicultural Urban Setting, (Spring 2008) Florida Educational Leadership Journal. Denise is also author of K-6 teacher handbooks on the topics of: Common Core ELA for Struggling Readers, Accelerating the Reading Achievement of Students with Learning Disabilities, Response to Intervention, Response to Intervention/Reading Assessment, and Co-Teaching

Additionally, during the past fifteen years, her focus has also included working with teachers to provide the most successful environment for high quality teaching experiences.

You will leave this seminar inspired and touched by Denise's enthusiasm, along with practical and highly effective strategies and a renewed sense of professional growth… insights and practical strategies you'll be able to use immediately.

Dedicated to Josh, Buffy, Matt, Annie, Zach, Diana, Kaylee, & Andy for their constant support & inspiration…

to Kaylee, who deserves to have the best teachers out there…

and to all exemplary teachers, who believe that we <u>must</u> build literacy connections for all learners.

Dear Colleagues,

The adoption of a Common Core Curriculum Standards gives educators hope that all students will have the opportunity to be taught robust standards based on the requirements of "tomorrow's students," while teaching consistent standards with consistent high expectations. It is a win-win framework for both our students and teachers.

To alleviate teachers' most common fear, "I won't be able to teach what I know is right," we'll look at work from the Common Core State Standards Initiatives, which states, "The Standards leave room for teachers, curriculum developers and states to determine how those goals should be reached and what additional topics should be addressed … teachers are thus free to provide students with whatever tools and knowledge their professional judgment and experience identify as most helpful for meeting the goals set out in the Standards." The second most common fear, "Do I have to change everything I've been doing?" will be explored as we examine your own standards and how they fit into the new and improved framework.

It is my goal that you leave my seminar with a plethora of strategies and an action plan to successfully implement these standards into your classroom. I look forward to meeting you and sharing my knowledge and experiences during our day together. I encourage you to attend in teams from your school if at all possible. It will be a bonus for you and your colleagues to work together toward a common goal! However, whether you attend alone or in a team, we will work collaboratively to reach and teach our students and embrace the new teaching and learning experiences of the Common Core Standards for Reading.

Sincerely,

Denise M. Gudwin

Denise Gudwin, Ph.D.

P.S. You will also receive an extensive resource handbook filled with numerous ideas and valuable practical strategies you can use immediately to assist you in aligning your reading instruction with the Common Core State Standards. If you would like further consultative services or information, please don't hesitate to contact me.

The essence of teaching is to make the learning contagious, to have one idea spark another.
                                                                                Marva Collins

Denise M. Gudwin Presents
a Comprehensive One-Day Seminar:

| Practical Strategies for Meeting the Rigorous Common Core State Standards for Reading (Grades K-2): A Teacher Handbook – Professional Development Series |

Denise M. Gudwin, Ph.D.

TABLE OF CONTENTS

	Introduction, Agenda, Expectations, Where Do We Begin	1
I	Common Core Standards: Background, Key Points, and What They Are/What They Are Not	5
II	Unwrapping or Unpacking the Common Core Standards – Grade Group Collaboration	10
III	Compare and Align the Successful Reading Strategies You Currently Use to the Common Core Reading Standards	16
IV	Implementing the Common Core Reading Standards in Your Classroom: Sample Lessons	17
V	Eight Ways to Manage and Organize Your Daily Reading Program to Support the Attainment of the Common Core Standards	36
VI	Accelerate Reading Through the Gradual Release of Responsibility Model	43
VII	Lessons Learned... How Do These Two Studies Connect to the Common Core Standards?	46
VIII	Additional Strategies	
	☐ Effective Strategies – What Do Good Readers Do? Teaching Higher Order Thinking Through Think Alouds, Literature Circles, Mentor Texts	48
	☐ Reading Standards for Literature (RL.K.2, RL.1.2, RL.2.2, RL.K.7, RL.1.7, RL.2.7) Read and Retell, Making Connections, Character Analysis, Compare and Contrast, Background Knowledge, My Favorite Children's Books For This Standard	54
	☐ Reading Standards for Informational Text (RI.K.5, RI.1.5, RI.2.5, RI.K.6, RI.1.6, RI.2.6) Book Walk/Book Talk, Picture Walk/Picture Talk, Genre Study, 6-Point-Story-Board, Self-Monitoring Metacognitive Strategies, My Favorite Children's Books For This Standard	57
	☐ Reading Standards: Foundational Skills – Phonics and Word Recognition (FS.K.3, FS.1.3, FS.2.3) Onset and Rime, Guess the Covered Word, Be a Mind Reader, Sorting Word Cards Into Patterns and Transfer, Rounding Up the Rhymes, My Favorite Children's Book For This Standard	60

© Denise M. Gudwin www.denise.gudwin.org

		Reading Standards: Foundational Skills – Fluency (FS.K.4, FS.1.4, FS.2.4) Fluency Cards, Fluency Chunk, Rereading – Ways to Bring Fun Into Fluency Practice, Word-by-Word Reading, My Favorite Children's Books For This Standard -----------------------------	62
		Speaking and Listening Standards – Comprehension and Collaboration (SL.K.1 ,SL.1.1, SL.2.1) Engage Your Students in Meaningful Talk, Collaborative Conversations (SL.K.4, SL.1.4, SL.2.4) Build a Story, Talk to Your Students, Telling Our Story Before Hearing the Author's Story, My Favorite Children's Books For This Standard ---	65
		Language Standards – Vocabulary Acquisition and Use (L.K.5a and L.K.5d, L.1.5a and L.1.5d, L.2.5a and L.2.5b) List-Group-Label, Sort and Describe, Word Collections, Linear Arrays, My Favorite Children's Books For This Standard ------------------------------	71
IX	Think About It: Reflections, Strategies, Expectations, Bottom Line -------------		74
X	Resources		
		Online Resources --	78
		Children's Books Referenced To the Standards Today ---------------	82
		References --	88
		Appendix --	96
		Reflective Note Pages ---	138
		Ongoing TO-DO List ---	140

It appears that the debate over the merits of establishing common standards is over. It is no longer considered acceptable that students in different states are learning at different levels. Kendall, 2011

Probably all of you have put some thought into the new Common Core Standards; some of you may love the new focus and some of you may even be dreading the shift – but today, we will explore the benefits of the Common Core and look forward to utilizing this framework to enhance our instructional practices.

I will share practical, ready-to-use tools and highly effective strategies you can use to focus your reading instruction. I will share efficient ways to help you manage your reading program to better support the Common Core. Kudos to you who have started to embrace this change – you are a resource to our seminar today: As some of you are just beginning this work, and others who have already started, we will collaborate to pave the way for success in your planning.

The idea that what teachers know and do, will influence what students know and do, is well confirmed (Florida Center for Reading Research). I hope that today's seminar, **Practical Strategies for Meeting the Rigorous Common Core State Standards for Reading (Grades K-2)** provides you with practical tools to take back... strategies, resources, and ideas that you can implement in your classroom or share with your colleagues right away. I look forward to working collaboratively with you today.

> "Would you tell me, please,
> which way I ought to go from here?"
> "That depends a good deal on
> where you want to get to," said the Cat.
> "I don't much care where –" said Alice.
> "Then it doesn't matter which way you go,"
> said the Cat.
> Lewis Carroll
> *Alice's Adventures in Wonderland*

Seminar Agenda

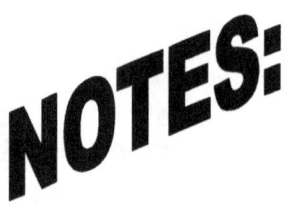

8:30 am to 3:15 pm

Practical Strategies for Meeting the Rigorous *Common Core State Standards* for Reading (Grades K-2): A Teacher Handbook – Professional Development Series

Dr. Denise M. Gudwin

Morning	Background Information
	Exploring the Resources
	Outstanding Reading Strategies Using the Standards
Lunch	11:30 am – 12:45 pm
Afternoon	Outstanding Reading Strategies Using the Standards
	Connecting the Dots

Action Planning and Reflection throughout the day… and, for your convenience, there will be a 10-minute break in the morning and again in the afternoon.

Please feel free to come talk to me during break or lunchtime. I'm happy to assist you in your learning journey. You may also contact me at a later time via email: denisegudwinconsulting@gmail.com or through my website at: www.denise.gudwin.org.

> The essence of teaching
> is to make learning contagious,
> to have one idea spark another.
> Marva Collins

How To Use This Resource Handbook

1. Write in it!
   Use the NOTES margin to write your thoughts, notes, and reflections. This will assist you when you refer to this handbook at a later time. Two excellent teaching strategies are applied by using your margin notes: Engaging with text and 2 column notes
2. Use Sticky Note Tabs on your favorite pages, for easy rereading.
3. Think Along: Think how <u>you</u> can apply this information to <u>your own</u> classroom and/or school.
   - What is being discussed at the seminar
   - What you read on your own
4. Highlight it in. Underline, circle, draw arrows, draw pictures… stimulate your brain; use your visual capacity to help you remember this seminar!

Jot down your reflections here – where you can easily refer to them.

Why Are We Here?

"Zip codes might be great for sorting mail, but they should not determine the quality of a child's education or success in the future workforce. With common standards and assessments, students, parents, and teachers will have a clear, consistent understanding of the skills necessary for students to succeed after high school and compete with peers across the state line and across the ocean."

Bob Wise, President, Alliance for Excellent Education and former Governor

What are our Collective Goals and Expectations for Today?

Why am I here today?
What do I want to take back with me?

1. _____
2. _____
3. _____
4. _____
5. _____

One of my goals with you today is to help solidify your above goals and expectations, and encourage you to further continue (over the next few months) to ask the questions:
- What do I need to be successful?
- What do my students need to be successful?
- What am I missing?
- Who can help me?
- How will I achieve my goals?
- What, exactly, are my goals?
- When will this all make sense?

Where Do We Begin?

Think of your students –
What are their weaknesses in reading?

- _____
- _____
- _____
- _____
- _____

What have you experienced in the "Standards" world?
And... What are the Common Core State Standards?

NOTES:

Let's take a moment to reflect and share:
What are four of the skills/standards that you have taught in Reading during the past few months?

1. _____
2. _____
3. _____
4. _____

I. Common Core Standards: Background, Key Points, and What They Are/ What They Are Not

Douglas Reeves (2010) shares five essential actions to use while planning your implementation of the Common Core:

1. **Find Common Ground**
    a. Look for similarities between your current curriculum and the Common Core.
    b. Highlight the ones you are already teaching.
    c. You can build on the successful strategies you will continue to use.
2. **More Informational Writing**
    a. One of Reeve's personal favorites – including informational writing across the subjects.
    b. Strong connection with non-fiction writing and student success.
    c. Make a commitment to increase. informational writing starting in kindergarten
    d. Writing – reading – thinking critically are all connected and developmentally appropriate for all grades.
3. **Prioritize**
    a. More than just delivering binders to your door.
    b. Take time to get to know the standards and identify the evidence of mastery.
    c. Collaborate to identify the most important standards that have the greatest impact on

your students' learning; sometimes called power standards.
4. **Embrace Common Formative Assessments at the District Level**
   a. Previous assessments were inconsistent with curriculum.
   b. Formative assessments are designed to inform teaching and learning.
5. **Use the Standards as a Floor, Not a Ceiling**
   a. Not a standardization of teaching and learning.
   b. Create a continuum of learning activities that include the requirements as well as opportunities to exceed them.
   c. Embrace teacher creativity.
   d. Start preparing now, even if your state has not finalized the preparation for implementation or assessment.

Our professional learning today is centered around these essential actions.

**College and Career Readiness
Common Core State Standards Initiative**

Key Points:

4 Strands
1. Reading – Our Focus Today
2. Writing
3. Speaking/Listening
4. Language

Organization

Each anchor standard has an accompanying grade-specific standard. RI.2.1 stands for **R**eading, **I**nformational Text (**RI**.2.1), grade **2** (RI.**2**.1), standard **1** (RI.2.**1**), "Ask and answer such questions as *who, what, where, when, why,* and *how* to demonstrate understanding of key details in a text."

Likewise, SL.K.1a represents **S**peaking and **L**istening (**SL**.K.1a), **k**indergarten (SL.**K**.1a), standard **1a** (SL.K.**1a**), "Follow agreed-upon rules for discussions (e.g., listening to others and taking turns speaking about the topics and texts under discussion)."

Text Complexity

Corestandards.org provides us valuable information in their Appendix A and Appendix B at: www.corestandards.org/assets/Appendix_A.pdf. and www.corestandards.org/assets/Appendix_B.pdf.
Three criteria were used in the process of text selection: 1) **Complexity**, using qualitative, quantitative, and professional judgment on matching readers and texts with regard to the particular tasks. 2) **Quality** – the work group selected texts of recognized value, considered classic or historically significant, as well as contemporary works of cultural significance – all with rich content. 3) **Range** – broad representation of sufficiently complex high quality texts, appropriate to the band of levels, with factors such as initial publication date, authorship, and subject matter considered.

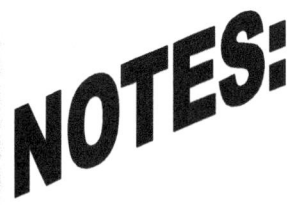

The figure below is from Appendix A (Figure 3) at www.corestandards.org.

Text Complexity Grade Band in the Standards	Old Lexile Ranges	Lexile Ranges Aligned to CCR Expectations
K-1	N/A	N/A
2-3	450-725	450-790
4-5	645-845	770-980

Grade-by-Grade Staircase

"The Reading standards place equal emphasis on the sophistication of what students read and the skill with which they read. Standard 10 defines a grade-by-grade 'staircase' of increasing text complexity that rises from beginning reading to the college and career readiness level. Whatever they are reading, students must also show a steadily growing ability to discern more from and make fuller use of text, including **making an increasing number of connections among ideas and between texts, considering a wider range of textual evidence, and becoming more sensitive to inconsistencies, ambiguities, and poor reasoning in texts**."

http://www.corestandards.org/the-standards/english-language-arts-standards/introduction/how-to-read-the-standards/

© Gudwin, D. www.denise.gudwin.org

A Focus on Results Rather Than Means

"By emphasizing required achievements, the Standards leave room for teachers, curriculum developers, and states to determine how those goals should be reached and what additional topics should be addressed. Thus, the Standards do not mandate such things as a particular writing process or the full range of metacognitive strategies that students may need to monitor and direct their thinking and learning. **Teachers are thus free to provide students with whatever tools and knowledge their professional judgment and experience identify as most helpful for meeting the goals set out in the standards.**"

http://www.corestandards.org/the-standards/english-language-arts-standards/introduction/key-design-considerations/

An Integrated Model of Literacy

"Although the Standards are divided into Reading, Writing, Speaking and Listening, and Language strands for conceptual clarity, the processes of communication are closely connected, as reflected throughout this document. For example, Writing standard 9 requires students be able to write about what they read. Likewise, Speaking and Listening standard 4 sets the expectation that students will share findings from their research."

http://www.corestandards.org/the-standards/english-language-arts-standards/introduction/key-design-considerations/

"The Standards aim to align instruction with this framework [the framework for the 2009 National Assessment of Educational Progress] so that many more students than at present can meet the requirements of college and career readiness. In K-5, the Standards follow NAEP's lead in balancing the reading of literature with the reading of **informational texts**, including texts in history/social studies, science, and technical subjects."

What is Not Covered by the Standards

1. "The Standards define what all students are expected to know and be able to do, **not how teachers should teach**. For instance, the use of play with young children is not specified by the Standards, but it is welcome as a valuable activity in its own right and as a way to help students meet the expectations in this document."

2. "While the Standards focus on what is most essential, they **do not describe all that can or should be taught**."
3. "The Standards **do not define the nature of advanced work** for students who meet the Standards prior to the end of high school. For these students, advanced work…should be available."
4. "The Standards set grade-specific standards but **do not define the intervention methods or materials necessary to support students** who are well below or well above grade-level expectations. No set of grade-specific standards can fully reflect the great variety in abilities, needs, learning rates, and achievement levels of students in any given classroom. However, the Standards do provide clear signposts along the way to the goal of college and career readiness for all students."
5. **"It is also beyond the scope of the Standards to define the full range of supports appropriate for English language learners and for students with special needs.** At the same time, all students must have the opportunity to learn and meet the same high standards if they are to access the knowledge and skills necessary in their post-high school lives… **The Standards should also be read as allowing for the widest possible range of students to participate fully from the outset and as permitting appropriate accommodations to ensure maximum participation of students with special education needs**. For example, for students with disabilities, *reading* should allow for the use of Braille, screen-reader technology, or other assistive devices, while *writing* should include the use of a scribe, computer, or speech-to-text technology. In a similar vein, *speaking and listening* should be interpreted broadly to include sign language."
6. "Students require a wide-ranging, rigorous academic preparation and, **particularly in the early grades, attention to such matters as social, emotional, and physical development and approaches to learning**."

Source: http://www.corestandards.org/the-standards/english-language-arts-standards/introduction/key-design-considerations/

The National Center for Learning Disabilities is pleased to support the Common Core Standards. We applaud and appreciate the work of the NGA and CCSSO and the expectation that all students can achieve high standards and become college and/or career ready. We are prepared to support families, teachers, schools and states as they strive to help all students succeed."
James H. Wendorf, Executive Director,
National Center for Learning Disabilities

II. Let's Look at Unwrapping or Unpacking the Common Core Standards

Teacher:
"Yes, but... I don't have time to unpack the standards. I am too busy ..."

Jackson, R. (2009):
"As important as it is, unpacking the standards does take some time... Taking the time to unpack the standards will actually help you be more efficient... You don't have to unpack them all at once... start to think differently and more strategically about how you teach and the learning activities you use."

" 'Unwrapping' the academic content standards is a proven technique to help educators identify from the full text of the standards exactly what they need to teach their students. Unwrapped standards provide clarity as to what students must know and be able to do. **When teachers take the time to analyze each standard and identify its essential concepts and skills, the result is more effective instructional planning, assessment, and student learning**" (Ainsworth, L., 2003).

"Once your targeted standards are unwrapped, what's the next step? **It is to help students realize why these**

NOTES:

concepts and skills are important for them to learn" (Ainsworth, L., 2003).

Weber (2008) shared that unpacking the standards can improve continuity for students between grades and provides increased opportunities for curriculum integration. It also helps teachers and administrators determine what matters most.

Let's delve deeper into Ainsworth's idea of *Unwrapping the Standards* with just one example. You may not choose to do this for every Standard, but it's a good way to look at one sample together!

1. Code It
2. Unwrap It
3. Determine the Big Ideas
4. Develop Essential Questions
5. Identify Facts, Concepts, Skills, Background Knowledge Needed

Choose your grade group…

Step 1 – Code It! – Highlight or underline the verbs and then highlight or circle the nouns:
Kindergarten Teachers:
   Standard **RL.K.2:** With prompting and support, retell familiar stories, including key details.

1st Grade Teachers:
   Standard **RL.1.2:** Grade 1 students will retell stories, including key details, and demonstrate understanding of their central message or lesson.

2nd Grade Teachers:
   Standard **RL.2.2:** Grade 2 students will recount stories, including fable and folktales from diverse cultures, and determine their central message, lesson, or moral.

3rd Grade + Teachers:
   Standard **RL.3.2:** Grade 3 students will recount stories, including fables, folktales, and myths from diverse cultures; determine the central message, lesson, or moral and explain how it is conveyed through key details in the text.

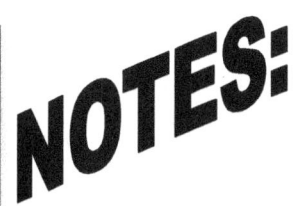

Before we move to Step 2, let's look at the differences in the staircase of grade level standards… it's so important to know where our students are headed – start with the end in mind. Think back to the Alice in Wonderland quote on page 1!

Step 2 – Unwrap It! – Identify the concepts and skills in the standard, to determine what students need to understand and do… You may want to rewrite to help them stand out.

Kindergarten Teachers:
   Break it up into smaller, more manageable parts: Standard **RL.K.2:** With prompting and support, retell familiar stories, including key details.

1st Grade Teachers:
   Break it up into smaller, more manageable parts: Standard **RL.1.2:** Grade 1 students will retell stories, including key details, and demonstrate understanding of their central message or lesson.

2nd Grade Teachers:
   Break it up into smaller, more manageable parts: Standard **RL.2.2:** Grade 2 students will recount stories, including fable and folktales from diverse cultures, and determine their central message, lesson, or moral.

3rd Grade + Teachers:
   Break it up into smaller, more manageable parts: Standard **RL.3.2:** Grade 3 students will recount stories, including fables, folktales, and myths from diverse cultures; determine the central message, lesson, or moral and explain how it is conveyed through key details in the text.

Step 3 – Determine the Big Ideas… What do they need to already know? What type of literacy skills will they need to use? Is this important for my students to learn?

Need to Know	Skills to Use	How will this help my students?

Kindergarten Teachers:
Standard **RL.K.2**: With prompting and support, retell familiar stories, including key details.

1st Grade Teachers:
Standard **RL.1.2**: Grade 1 students will retell stories, including key details, and demonstrate understanding of their central message or lesson.

2nd Grade Teachers:
Standard **RL.2.2**: Grade 2 students will recount stories, including fable and folktales from diverse cultures, and determine their central message, lesson, or moral.

3rd Grade + Teachers:
Standard **RL.3.2**: Grade 3 students will recount stories, including fables, folktales, and myths from diverse cultures; determine the central message, lesson, or moral and explain how it is conveyed through key details in the text.

Grade Group Reflections for Steps 2 and 3

Step 4 – Write at least one essential question derived from the unwrapped standard and the big idea. Engage your students in the process and take them beyond the basic who, what, when, where, I liked it because…

Question	Question

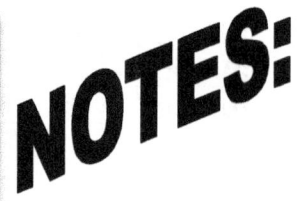

Kindergarten Teachers:
   Standard **RL.K.2:** With prompting and support, retell familiar stories, including key details.

1st Grade Teachers:
   Standard **RL.1.2:** Grade 1 students will retell stories, including key details, and demonstrate understanding of their central message or lesson.

2nd Grade Teachers:
   Standard **RL.2.2:** Grade 2 students will recount stories, including fable and folktales from diverse cultures, and determine their central message, lesson, or moral.

3rd Grade + Teachers:
   Standard **RL.3.2:** Grade 3 students will recount stories, including fables, folktales, and myths from diverse cultures; determine the central message, lesson, or moral and explain how it is conveyed through key details in the text.

Grade Group Reflections for Step 4

Step 5 – What will my students need to do, to demonstrate an understanding of this standard? What facts should they know, what concepts should they understand, and what skills should they use?

Facts they should know	Concepts they should understand	Skills they should use

NOTES:

Kindergarten Teachers:
Standard **RL.K.2:** With prompting and support, retell familiar stories, including key details.

1st Grade Teachers:
Standard **RL1.2.:** Grade 1 students will retell stories, including key details, and demonstrate understanding of their central message or lesson.

2nd Grade Teachers:
Standard **RL2.2:** Grade 2 students will recount stories, including fable and folktales from diverse cultures, and determine their central message, lesson, or moral.

3rd Grade + Teachers:
Standard **RL3.2:** Grade 3 students will recount stories, including fables, folktales, and myths from diverse cultures; determine the central message, lesson, or moral and explain how it is conveyed through key details in the text.

Grade Group Reflections for Step 5

Did this activity make sense to you?

"Our best understanding
of what works in our schools
comes from the teachers who teach
in our classrooms every day.
That is why these standards
establish what students need to learn,
but do not dictate how teachers should teach.
Instead, the standards enable schools
and teachers to decide how best
to help students reach the standards."
Dr. Eric J. Smith. Florida Commissioner of Education

III. Compare and Align the Successful Reading Strategies You Currently Use to the Common Core Reading Standards

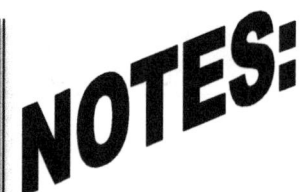

Let's do a Standards' Walk-Through (See Appendix, p. 99-113)

Guiding question #1: **Do you see familiar language?**
Jot down one or two words…

Reading Standards for Literature (RL)	
Reading Standards for Informational Text (RI)	
Reading Standards: Foundational Skills (FS)	
Speaking and Listening Standards (SL)	
Language Standards (L)	

Guiding question #2: **Do you see skills/standards in the Standards that you currently teach in Reading?**
Jot down a few…

Reading Standards for Literature (RL)	
Reading Standards for Informational Text (RI)	
Reading Standards: Foundational Skills (FS)	
Speaking and Listening Standards (SL)	
Language Standards (L)	

© Gudwin, D. www.denise.gudwin.org

> "Common standards ensure that every child across the country is getting the best possible education, no matter where a child lives or what their background is. The common standards will provide an accessible roadmap for schools, teachers, parents and students, with clear and realistic goals."
> Gov. Roy Romer, Senior Advisor, The College Board

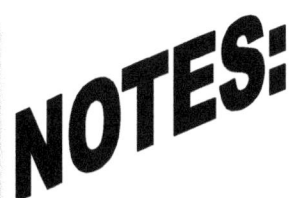

IV. Implementing the Common Core Reading Standards in Your Classroom

Let's walk through another Reading Strand of specific Standards, which you can implement in your classroom.

	Kindergarten Students	**Grade 1 Students**	**Grade 2 Students**
Craft and Structure #6	**RL.K.6** **With prompting and support, name the author and illustrator** of a story and **define the role of each** in telling the story.	**RL.1.6** Identify **who is telling** the story **at various points** in a text.	**RL.2.6** Acknowledge **differences in the points of view of characters**, including by **speaking in a different voice for each character** when reading dialogue aloud.
	Where are our students going? **RL.3.6: Grade 3** – Distinguish **their own point of view** from that of the narrator or those of the characters. **RL.5.6: Grade 5** – Describe **how** a narrator or speaker's **point of view influences** how events as described.		

Possible lesson
- Purpose:

- Essential Questions, Background Knowledge needed, Skills to know beforehand:

- Strategies to teach:

- What about your struggling readers? Accommodations?

- What about your advanced readers? Enrichment?

- Anchor Charts:

"The Common Core Standards
just makes sense.
If a student moves from state to state,
they ought to know what the expectations are.
In teaching, we need to start with the end in mind…
in this case, the end in mind
is starting with K to 12
and the end being college and career ready."
Leah Luke, State Teacher of the Year Wisconsin

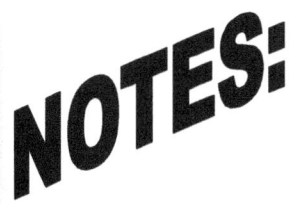

> **Two Sample Lessons** from
> **Common Core Curriculum Maps,**
> used with permission from
> www.commoncore.org/maps/unit/grade_k_unit_2
> and
> http://commoncore.org/maps/unit/grade_2_unit_3

Note: Some lessons are free, some require membership for a nominal fee.

Tell A Story, 1-2-3 (Kindergarten)

In this second six-week unit of kindergarten, students focus on sequence as they enjoy Counting Books, both fictional and information, and stories based on three.

Essential Question:
How are the beginning, the middle, and the end of a story different from each other?

Overview:
Building on the wide exposure to text types in the first unit, students now focus on the sequence of a text: the beginning, middle, and end of a story. They learn to retell rich stories and, by listening to versions of traditional stories, recognize familiar storylines embedded in different settings with different characters. Counting rhymes and reading a number of counting books will continue the first unit's focus on phonological awareness and listening for more rhythm and rhyme, as well as on sequencing. Students study three paintings, which are used for a creative storytelling activity and are related to the idea of multiple versions of a familiar story.

Focus Standards (These Focus Standards have been selected for the unit from the Common Core Standards):

- **RL.K.2** With prompting and support, retell familiar stories, including key details.

- **RL.K.9** With prompting and support, compare and contrast the adventures and experiences of characters in familiar stories.

- **RI.K.1** With prompting and support, ask and

answer questions about key details in a text.

- **SL.K.1** Participate in collaborative conversations with diverse partners about kindergarten topics and texts with peers and adults in small and larger groups.

- **SL.K.1b** Continue a conversation through multiple exchanges.

- **W.K.3** Use a combination of drawing, dictating, and writing to narrate a single event or several loosely linked events, tell about the events in the order in which they occurred, and provide a reaction to what happened.

- **L.K.2** Demonstrate command of the conventions of standard English capitalization, punctuation, and spelling when writing.

- **L.K.2a** Capitalize the first word in a sentence and the pronoun I.

Suggested Objectives:
- Name the author and illustrator of both the fictional and informational texts in this unit.
- Orally retell familiar stories, including details and events at the beginning, middle, and end.
- Recite and produce rhyming words from nursery rhymes and rhyming texts.
- Use a combination of writing, drawing, and dictating to retell stories with a beginning, middle, and end.
- Distinguish shades of meaning among simple adjectives.
- Recognize the importance of sequence in storytelling, information and fictional counting books, and nursery rhymes.
- Appreciate the difference between an original story and other versions of the same story.

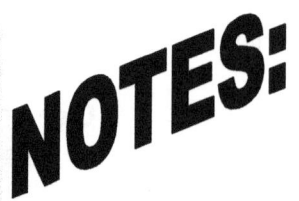

Suggested Works (Appropriate Texts):
The lesson also provides a large variety of texts (books, poems, nursery rhymes) some read aloud and some read along, as suggested for use:

Eight Nursery Rhymes	Literary
Six Picture Books	Literary – e.g., Chicka Chicka 1,2,3
Three Poems	Literary – e.g., Mix a Pancake
Thirteen Stories	Literary – e.g., Pancakes for Breakfast
Eleven Nonfiction	Informational – e.g., Beatrice's Goat

Note: (E) indicates a CCSS exemplar text; (EA) indicates a text from a writer with other works identified as exemplars.

Literary Texts

Nursery Rhymes
- "A Diller, A Dollar" (Read Along)
- "Baa, Baa, Black Sheep" (Read Along)
- "Hickory, Dickory, Dock" (Read Along)
- "Hot Cross Buns" (Read Along)
- "Old King Cole" (Read Along)
- "One, Two, Buckle My Shoe" (Read Along)
- "This Little Pig Went to Market" (Read Along)
- "Three Blind Mice" (Read Along)

Picture Books
- Anno's Counting Book (Mitsumasa Anno) (Read Aloud)
- Chicka Chicka 1, 2, 3 (Bill Martin, Jr., Michael Sampson, and Lois Ehlert) (Read Aloud)
- Grandfather Counts (Andrea Cheng) (Read Aloud)
- One Is a Snail, Ten Is a Crab: A Counting by Feet Book (April Pulley Sayre, Jeff Sayre, and Randy Cecil) (Read Aloud)
- Ten Apples Up on Top! (Dr. Seuss) (EA) (Read Aloud)
- Ten, Nine, Eight (Molly Bang) (EA) (Read Aloud)

Poems
- "Mix a Pancake" in The Complete Poems (Christina Rossetti) (E) (Read Along)
- "Three Little Kittens" in The Oxford Illustrated Book of American Children's Poems (Eliza Lee Follen) (Read Aloud)
- "Zin! Zin! Zin! A Violin" (Lloyd Moss and Marjorie Priceman) (E) (Read Aloud)

Stories
- Goldilocks and the Three Bears (Jan Brett) (Read Aloud)
- Horrible Harry Bugs the Three Bears (Suzy Kline and Frank Remkiewicz) (Read Aloud)
- Pancakes for Breakfast (Tomie DePaola) (E) (Read Along)
- Ten Black Dots (Donald Crews) (EA) (Read Along)
- The Three Billy Goats Gruff (Paul Galdone) (Read Aloud)
- The Three Cabritos (Eric A. Kimmel and Stephen Gilpin) (Read Aloud)
- The Three Little Javelinas: Los Tres Pequenos Jabalies (bilingual) (Susan Lowell) (Read Aloud)
- The Three Little Pigs (James Marshall) (Read Aloud)
- The Three Little Wolves and the Big Bad Pig (Eugene Trivizas and Helen Oxenbury) (Read Aloud)
- The Three Pigs (David Wiesner) (Read Aloud)
- The True Story of the Three Little Pigs (Jon Scieszka and Lane Smith) (Read Aloud)
- The Very Hungry Caterpillar (Eric Carle) (Read Along)
- Three Cool Kids (Rebecca Emberley) (Read Aloud)

Informational Texts
Nonfiction Books
- Arlene Alda's 1-2-3: What Do You See? (Arlene Alda) (Read Aloud)
- Beatrice's Goat (Page McBrier and Lori Lohstoeter) (Read Aloud)
- Can You Count Ten Toes? Count to Ten in Ten Different Languages (Lezlie Evans and Denis Roche) (Read Aloud)
- Farm Animals (Young Nature Series) (Felicity Everett) (Read Aloud)
- Goats (Animals That Live on the Farm) (JoAnn Early Macken) (Read Aloud)

- Moja Means One: Swahili Counting Book (Muriel and Tom Feelings) (Read Aloud)
- One Is a Drummer: A Book of Numbers (Roseanne Thong and Grace Lin) (Read Aloud)
- Our Animal Friends at Maple Hill Farm (Alice and Martin Provensen) (EA) (Read Aloud)
- Pigs (Animals That Live on the Farm) (JoAnn Early Macken) (Read Aloud)
- Pigs (Gail Gibbons) (EA) (Read Aloud)
- The Year at Maple Hill Farm (Alice and Martin Provensen) (E) (Read Aloud)

Art, Music, and Media
- Jean-Francois Millet, First Steps - www.vggallery.com/influences/millit/m_0668.htm (1858-1859)
- Pablo Picasso, Mother and Child, First Steps www.artgallery.yale.edu/pages/collection/popups/pc_modern/enlarge2.html (1943)
- Vincent van Gogh, First Steps, After Millet www.metmuseum.org/toah/works-of-art/64.165.2 (1890)

Sample Activities and Assessments (Possible Teaching and Learning Lessons and Activities):
Teacher Notes: Continue work on rhythm and rhyme from Unit One as more of the students show readiness to hear and see rhyming words. (**RF.K.2a**)

- **Reading Foundations, Informative Writing**
Create a counting book using the letters covered so far this year. Each student will choose a favorite letter and then brainstorm words that begin with that letter. Using the numbers one through five and five different things that begin with the chosen letter, create a book (e.g., *A Counting Book for T: 1 Tadpole, 2 Turkeys, 3 Toads, 4 Tigers, 5 Trout*). Title each student's book *A Counting Book for* _____. Be sure to write the name of the author and illustrator (student) on the cover of the book. Place the finished books in a basket for other students to enjoy. (**RF.K.1a, RF.K.1b, RF.K.1c, RF.K.1d, RF.K.3a**)

- **Art, Reading Poetry, Speaking and Listening**
"Mix a Pancake" is a poem written by Christina Rossetti. Have students draw illustrations that match the words to show the steps in making pancakes.

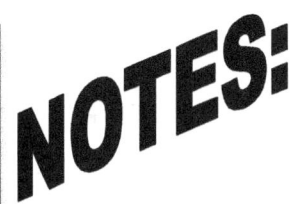

When finished, they can share the illustrations with a friend and read (recite) the poem together. (**RL.K.5, RL.K.7, W.K.2**)

- **Reading Literature, Language Usage**
Read the traditional version of a story first. Then read a different version of the story. For example, read the Galdone version of "The Three Billy Goats Gruff" and discuss the beginning, middle, and end of the story. Then read one of the other versions discussing how the beginning, middle, and end are similar, but also how the setting and characters make it a different story. Note how important the varied shades of meaning for action words (verbs) are crucial to each story. (**RL.K.9, L.K.5b**)

- **Reading Literature, Narrative Writing**
Using the book of illustrations *Pancakes for Breakfast* (Tomie DePaola), have students look at the illustrations and note how the pictures tell a story. Point out the importance of looking very closely at the details in the illustrations to tell what happens next. Encourage active thinking by asking what might happen when the page is turned to the next illustration. Because this is a wordless book, point out how the illustrator is telling a story without words. Even picture books with words tell a story through the illustrations. Write the students' dictated stories on sentence strips and place them in a pocket chart. Focus on modeling the capital letter required at the beginning of a sentence and the word I. (Extend this activity by reversing this process: read aloud the text of a simple book without showing the illustrations. Ask students to illustrate the story, creating their own wordless book. The students' illustrations can then be compared to the book.) (**RL.K.6, RL.K.5, RL.K.7, L.K.2a**)

- **Reading Informational Text, Research**
Because pigs and goats are talking characters who have personalities in these stories, students will enjoy reading about real pigs and goats. Beginning with books and digital resources on pigs or goats, keep a chart of animal needs that are met on the farm. Extend this work by writing a class book about real pigs or real goats. Be sure to talk about their needs and how those needs are met on farms. In an effort to pave the way for focused research, you may want to demonstrate the use of key word searches on a web browser with

an interactive whiteboard or other projection device. (**RI.K.1, RI.K.6, W.K.2, W.K.7, W.K.8**)

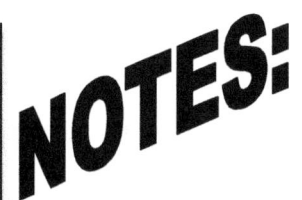

- **Narrative Writing**
Ask students to retell the story of *Goldilocks and the Three Bears.* Tell them to use illustrations, dictating, and/or writing. Tell them to be sure to focus on the beginning, middle, and end of the story by using transitional words (e.g., ordinal numbers: first, second, . . ."). You may use paper folded into three sections to help some students organize their ideas for the beginning, middle, and end. Encourage students to include all the characters in the story and to add as many details as they can remember. You may extend this writing activity for advanced students by asking them to write a new version of Goldilocks and the Three Bears. Be sure to have them change the characters and the setting and to illustrate the new story to create a class book. (**RL.K.1, RL.K.2, L.K.1a, L.K.1b, L.K.1c, L.K.2a, L.K.5b, W.K.3, W.K.5**)

- **Reading Informational Text, Speaking and Listening**
Tell students, "Today you will have to think, ask questions, and answer questions while we read an informational counting book titled *One Is a Drummer: A Book of Numbers* by Roseanne Thong and Grace Lin." (**RI.K.1, RI.K.6**)

- **Art, Opinion Writing**
Ask students to choose the painting they like best and to write (or dictate) a sentence saying why they chose that painting as their favorite. Remind them to begin their sentences with capital letters and to put periods at the end. (**W.K.1, W.K.3**)

- **Art, Speaking and Listening**
To introduce "versions" of a story to your class, use Millet's *First Steps* as the original "story." Allow the class to study the painting, giving plenty of time to notice details and create a possible story about the painting. Then show them van Gogh's First Steps, after Millet and have the class note how the "original characters are still in the story," but also that it all looks different (e.g., the Millet is in pencil while the van Gogh is an oil painting; in the Millet the people are prominent, whereas in the van Gogh, other elements—such as the gate, the wheelbarrow, and the tree—are also emphasized). Finally, show them Picasso's *First*

© Gudwin, D. www.denise.gudwin.org

Steps to see how another artist expressed the same idea in a completely different way. (**RL.K.9**)

- **Speaking and Listening, Language Usage**
Arrange small groups of students and place an object (e.g., a block) in the middle of the circle. As a class, tell the story of *Goldilocks and the Three Bears*, having students take turns telling the events in the story. Students pick up the block when ready to fill in part of the story and put the block back in the middle when finished. Encourage the students to identify all the characters and setting, as well as the major events of the story, when retelling. Encourage the students to note the importance of describing words (adjectives) in the telling of the story. For example, note the different ways the characters are described. Storytelling is shared with all the members of the group. (**RL.K.2, RL.K.3, SL.K.1a, SL.K.1b, L.K.5b**)

- **Art, Narrative Writing**
After looking closely at three paintings with the same title, *First Steps*, choose one of the paintings and imagine it shows the beginning of a story. Pair students to create the middle and end of the story to share with the class. Prompt: Choose one of the paintings and write (or dictate) a sentence telling why you chose that painting as your favorite. Be sure to begin your sentence with a capital letter and put a period at the end. (**W.K.1, W.K.3**)

A Pacing Guide For Reading Instruction
The Pacing Guides for Reading Foundations begin at a level appropriate for students who do not already know how to read. This will be the majority of students in most school systems, including those who enter school with limited language and/or literary experience and those who simply lack the phonological, decoding, and encoding skills needed for beginning reading and spelling. The pacing of code-emphasis instruction and the amount of time allotted to it will vary according to student skill levels, as measured on early screening, diagnostic, and progress-monitoring assessments. Nevertheless, all students need to master these essential building blocks.

Some students enter school having already learned the alphabetic principle and basic word recognition and are reading above expectation for these early grades. Those students should be allowed to progress more quickly through the foundational skills sequence, as long as they demonstrate mastery of the concepts. It is conceivable that in the same class, one group of students may just be finishing Level One at the end of the first kindergarten unit, but another group of students could be finishing Level Three at the end of the first kindergarten unit if the pace is accelerated.

At times, the content maps might seem incongruent with the skills in the Reading Foundations. An important fact about our maps is that the activities are simply "sample" activities. They represent a range of activities. Also, in keeping with the Common Core State Standards, we continually use developmental options for writing such as "using a combination of drawing, dictating, and writing."

Differentiated instruction is at the heart of effective classroom management. Teachers may need to deliver the literature-focused and content-focused part of the lesson by reading to and dialoguing with the students, taking care to ensure that they also teach a code-emphasis, explicit and systematic program to all those who need it.

Additional Resources

- Interview with Tomie DePaolo
  RL.K.6 (Reading Rockets)
  www.readingrockets.org/books/interviews/depaola

- Poetry Portfolios: Using Poetry to Teach Reading
  RL.K.5 (ReadWriteThink)
  www.readwritethink.org/classroom-resources/lesson-plans/poetry-portfolios-using-poetry-152.html

- Story Kit, a free application available from iTunes
  W.K.1., W.K.2, and/or **W.K.3**
  Itunes.apple.com/us/app/storykit/id329374595?mt=8

The website also provides terminology and interdisciplinary connections.

Used with permission: Common Core Curriculum Maps.
www.commoncore.org/maps/unit/grade_k_unit_2

This resource provides us quality choices to successfully differentiate instruction, based on our students needs. What resources might you add to this? What successful lessons do you love using and that your students respond to successfully?

Building Bridges with Unlikely Friends (Grade 2)

In this third six-week unit of second grade, students explore literal and figurative language through the theme of building bridges.

Essential Question:
Why do authors use figurative language?

Overview:
Students read informational (how-to) texts on building bridges and view these amazing structures on the Internet. Through realistic fiction, they examine the possibility of friendship in conflict-filled settings. Reading fantasy texts that depict animals' experiences with "bridge-building" completes their exploration. Building on the writing of previous units, they write a letter to a character in Charlotte's Web. Students also gather words from poetry and explore the meanings of idioms and words with common roots.

Focus Standards (These Focus Standards have been selected for the unit from the Common Core Standards):

- **RL.2.3**   Describe how characters in a story respond to major events and challenges.

- **RL.2.7**   Use information gained from the illustrations and words in a print or digital text to demonstrate understanding of its characters, setting, or plot.

- **RI.2.6**   Identify the main purpose of a text, including what the author wants to answer, explain, or describe.

- **W.2.2**   Write explanatory texts in which they introduce a topic, use facts and definitions to develop points, and provide a concluding statement or section.

- **L.2.2**   Demonstrate command of the conventions of standard English capitalization, punctuation, and spelling when writing.

- **L.2.2b**   Use commas in greetings and closing of letters.

- **L.2.4** Determine or clarify the meaning of unknown and multiple-meaning words and phrases based on Grade Two reading and content, choosing flexibly from an array of strategies.

- **L.2.4d** Use knowledge of the meaning of individual words to predict the meaning of compound words.

- NOTE: I would add **SL.2.1b**: *Build on others' talk in conversations by linking their comments to the remark of others* and **SL.2.2**: *Recount or describe key ideas or details from a text read aloud or information presented orally or through other media.*

Suggested Objectives:
- Read a how-to book.
- Write an explanatory piece on how to do something.
- Discern the difference between the use of literal and figurative language.
- Discern authors' techniques for describing characters.
- Write friendly letters to one of the characters in a book.
- Use commas correctly in the greeting and closing of a friendly letter.
- Write responses to a letter from a character's point of view.
- Use knowledge of a root word, such as bridge, to predict the meaning of compound words and idioms.
- Describe the use of riddles and other language in Haiku poetry.

Suggested Works (Appropriate Texts):
The lesson also provides a large list texts (books, poems, nursery rhymes) some read aloud and some read along, as suggested for use:

Three Poems	Literary – e.g., I Am the Dog, I Am the Cat
Fifteen Stories	Literary – e.g., Charlotte's Web
Six Nonfiction	Informational – e.g., Bridges Are To Cross

Note: (E) indicates a CCSS exemplar text; (EA) indicates a text from a writer with other works identified as exemplars.

Literary Texts

Poems
- "The Bridge Builder" (Will Allen Dromgoole) (Read Aloud)
- I Am the Dog I Am the Cat (Donald Hall) (Read Aloud)
- If Not for the Cat (Jack Prelutsky and Ted Rand) (Read Aloud)

Stories
- Charlotte's Web (E.B. White and Garth Williams) (E) (Read Aloud)
- Four Feet, Two Sandals (Karen Lynn Williams, Khadra Mohammed, and Doug Chayka) (Read Aloud)
- George and Martha: The Complete Stories of Two Best Friends (James Marshall)
- Henry and Mudge: The First Book (Cynthia Rylant and Sucie Stevenson) (E)
- Mackinac Bridge: The Story of the Five-Mile Poem (Gloria Whelan and Gijsbert van Frankenhuyzen) (Read Aloud)
- My Father's Shop (Satomi Ichikawa) (Read Aloud)
- One Green Apple (Eve Bunting and Ted Lewin) (EA) (Read Aloud)
- Pop's Bridge (Eve Bunting and C.F. Payne) (Read Aloud)
- Silent Music (James Rumford) (Read Aloud)
- Snow in Jerusalem (Deborah da Costa, Ying-Hwa Hu, and Cornelius Van Wright) (Read Aloud)
- The Cricket in Times Square (George Selden and Garth Williams) (E) (Read Aloud)
- The Day of Ahmed's Secret (Florence P. Heide, Judith H. Gilliland and Ted Lewin) (Read Aloud)
- The Fire Cat (Esther Holden Averill) (E)
- The Little Painter of Sabana Grande (Patricia Maloney Markun and Robert Casilla) (Read Aloud)
- Zen Shorts (Jon J. Muth) (Read Aloud)

Informational Texts
Nonfiction Books
- Bridges (See More Readers) (Seymour Simon) (EA)
- Bridges Are To Cross (Philemon Sturges and Giles Laroche) (Read Aloud)

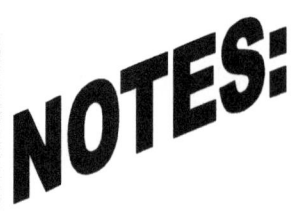

- Bridges: Amazing Structures to Design, Build & Test (Carol A. Johmann, Elizabeth Rieth, and Michael P. Kline) (Read Aloud)
- Owen and Mzee: The Language of Friendship (Isabella and Craig Hatkoff, Paula Kahumbu, and Peter Greste) (Read Aloud)
- Owen and Mzee: The True Story of a Remarkable Friendship (Isabella and Craig Hatkoff, Paula Kahumbu, and Peter Greste) (Read Aloud)
- Tarra and Bella: The Elephant and Dog Who Became Best Friends (Carol Buckley) (Read Aloud)

Art, Music, and Media
- Album Quilt
www.philamuseum.org/collections/permanent/138009.html   (New York, 1853)
- Album Quilts
www.artbma.org/collection/overview/decorative.html (Maryland, ca. 1840)

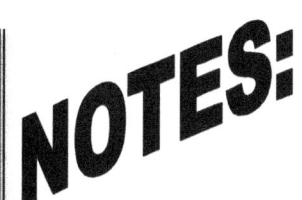

Sample Activities and Assessments (Possible Teaching and Learning Lessons and Activities):
- Teacher Notes: This unit could be taught in three parts. First, start with "bridges" so that students see the bridge as both an architectural structure and a symbolic metaphor coming together. Students will then see how children are able to bridge cultural gaps through friendship. Then read the fictional works to further the theme of Unlikely Friends. Students will think about differences in characters such as Charlotte and Wilbur and the way they become friends. Finally, writing a friendly letter to a book character will help the students to think deeply about the fictional characters.

- **Reading Literature, Speaking and Listening**
Introduce a book such as Snow in Jerusalem (Deborah da Costa, Ying-Hwa Hu, and Cornelius Van Wright) by reviewing how unlikely friends become friends by finding something in common. Tell the students that they are going to read a book about two children who were not friends but who found something in common anyway. As they read the story have the students focus on how the children find something in common to make a friendship. Talk about how these two characters faced a challenge and made a hard choice. **(RL.2.3, RL.2.7)**

- **Art, Speaking and Listening**
  Use the Philadelphia Museum of Art and Baltimore Museum of Art's websites to explore the tradition of album quilts. Discuss with students the reasons behind making such quilts. How would quilting build strong friendships? What types of images do you see in these quilts? What do the images tell us about the people who made these quilts? (**SL.2.4**)

- **Art, Speaking and Listening**
  Using paper squares and cut-out images, divide the class into (unlikely) groupings of three to four students. Have them discuss what type of album quilt they would like to produce as a group—what event should they commemorate? Using teamwork, each group should produce a small "quilt" of images. (**SL.2.1, SL.2.5**)

- **Narrative Writing**
  To encourage communication among unlikely friends, arrange for your students to communicate with students from another class in a place far away. Begin an e-mail or pen-pal correspondence with students from another class in a contrasting location. Setting parameters for what can be shared, ask students to write letters introducing themselves and asking the other student about him/herself. The purpose of this activity would be to find ways the students are similar and the ways the students are different from one another. This writing activity could also be done writing from whole class to whole class instead of students writing to one another. (**W.2.6, W.2.5, L.2.2b**)

- **Reading Literature, Narrative Writing**
  Read aloud the book Charlotte's Web (E. B. White) to the class. After you have finished the book, have the students connect with the characters in the book by writing friendly letters. Students should choose one of the characters in Charlotte's Web and write the character a letter. You may say, "Write a letter to one of the characters in Charlotte's Web. Explain why you chose the character, what you like about him or her, and ask the character a question." Require proper use of punctuation and form for the letters. Revise the letters and edit for spelling and punctuation. Then, have the students trade letters and write back to a classmate as if they were the classmate's chosen character. For example, if a child receives a letter

addressed to Wilbur, she would write a letter back as if she were Wilbur and answer the question asked. **(L.2.2b, RL.2.7, W.2.5)**

- **Reading Informational Text, Language Usage**
  After reading about bridges, have students predict the meaning of compound words that contain the word "bridge:" footbridge, drawbridge, flybridge, and bridgework. Repeat the activity using another root word such as water: waterbed, watercolor, watermelon, waterlog, watershed, waterproof, watertight, rainwater, waterway, and waterspout. Extend this lesson by discussing idioms using the word bridge such as "We'll cross that bridge when we come to it," "that's water under the bridge," and "don't burn your bridges." **(L.2.4d)**

- **Reading Informational Text, Informative Writing, Speaking and Listening**
  Begin a class discussion by asking the students: "If a real hippopotamus had no other companions, what other kind of animal could you imagine her having for a friend?" Be sure to require good reasons for their opinions as they answer. Read the book Owen and Mzee: The True Story of a Remarkable Friendship (Isabella Hatkoff) aloud. When you are finished reading, have the students discuss what the author (a six-year-old girl) wanted to accomplish by publishing the book, using questions such as: "What did she want to explain? Describe? What questions did she want to answer? Why are there so many photographs?" Ask students to write a paragraph explaining how the two animals in the story became friends. Writing prompt: "After reading about these unlikely friends (i.e., Owen and Mzee), write a paragraph explaining how the two animals in the story became friends." **(SL.2.6, W.2.2, RI.2.6, RI.2.3, RI.2.7)**

- **Reading Informational Text, Informative Writing**
  Introduce a chapter from Bridges: Amazing Structures to Design, Build, and Test. This is an informational book, but it is also a how-to book. It will teach how to build bridge structures in the classroom or at home. Read the text to the children and allow them to note that the how-to section is set up as a series of steps to follow. Gather the supplies and allow the students to follow the directions to experiment with building a bridge. Discuss how diagrams help to explain the

directions. Writing prompt: "After building a bridge in the classroom or at home, write an explanatory paragraph telling someone else how you made your bridge." (**SL.2.6, W.2.2, RI.2.6, RI.2.3, RI.2.7**)

- **Reading Poetry, Vocabulary, Speaking and Listening**
  As you read from the poetry collection If Not for the Cat (Jack Prelutsky), explain to students the Haiku style of poetry. Point out to the students that these poems are very short, but they make you think. As you read a poem, keep the accompanying illustration hidden until students try to guess the animal being described. These poems are filled with words that may be new to your students. When you are finished reading (reciting) each poem, ask students to choose one new word to save in the word bank. (**L.2.4e, L.2.5, RL.2.4**)

- **Reading Literature, Speaking and Listening**
  As students read the Henry and Mudge books, challenge them to look closely at the characters. Before the first chapter, ask the students to be ready to describe Henry and Mudge. Using sticky notes or whiteboards, require each student to write down two characteristics of each character. Although one of the characters is a dog and one is a boy, they have a wonderful friendship. Have students share at least two words to describe Henry and two words to describe Mudge. Discuss what can be learned about friendship through these stories. (**RL.2.7, L.2.5b**)

- **Reading Literature, Speaking and Listening**
  Introduce the idea of a bridge as a metaphor by reading the book Pop's Bridge (Eve Bunting). (Help the students think of more metaphors to reinforce the meaning of this important term.) In this book, a group of boys experience the sacrifice involved in bridge building and the joy that comes with friendship. Discuss the literal bridge in the book and the way the bridge served as a link not only between two places, but also between two people. Introduce the following Isaac Newton quotation: "We build too many walls and not enough bridges." Discuss what Isaac Newton may have meant by his comment. (**RL.2.7**)

Additional Resources
- Fun and Learning About Bridges
  RI.2.3
  www.bridgesite.com/funand.htm

- Letter Generator
  W.2.6, L.2.2b (ReadWriteThink)
  http://www.readwritethink.org/parent-afterschool-resources/games-tools/letter-generator-a-30187.html

- Friendly Letter Mini-Lesson
  L.2.2b
  www.lesn.appstate.edu/fryeem/RE4030.friendly_letter_minilesson.htm

The website also provides terminology and interdisciplinary connections.

Used with permission: Common Core Curriculum Maps.
http://commoncore.org/maps/unit/grade_2_unit_3

This resource provides us quality choices to successfully differentiate instruction, based on our students needs. What resources might you add to this? What successful lessons do you love using and that your students respond to successfully?

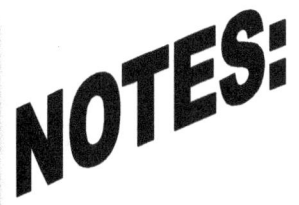

> "If we use these common standards
> as the foundation for better schools,
> we can give all kids a robust curriculum
> taught by well-prepared, well-supported teachers
> who can help prepare them for success in college,
> life and careers."
> Randi Weingarten, President, American Federation of Teachers

V. Eight Ways to Manage and Organize Your Daily Reading Program to Support the Attainment of the Common Core Standards

NOTES:

1. **Unpack the Standards**
   - Get together as a grade group over food/drink in a comfortable setting.
   - Discuss whether a pacing guide would work for you/your grade level.
   - Explore your existing state standards. How are they different? How are the similar? What do you want to keep? What can you let go? What do you want to add?
   - Prioritize your focus standards – knowing your students' levels and background.
   - Develop your essential questions for each lesson.
   - What is your State, your District, your School-Site Administrator requiring you to do?
   - Organize them in a binder, or on a wall chart, or on a spreadsheet attached to a clipboard, or use them online… whatever works for you, as you get familiar with the information.

2. **Examine what you already teach**
   - The strategies that you find incredibly successful – do they fit in with the Standards? Where?
   - If you could make changes to your classroom instruction, what would that include?
   - Do you agree with high expectations, scaffolding, and guided support?
   - Are the majority of your students demonstrating academic success?
   - Are you using Differentiated Instruction strategies every day?
   - Look at the Four Cs: Collaboration, Communication, Creativity, and Critical Thinking… What are you currently "doing" with the Four Cs? And… What do you need to do differently?

3. **Alternate whole group with small groups**, at 10-25 minute intervals. Try to work with no more than three

small groups a day, even if you have 4 or 5 small groups. Whole groups can include grade-level shared reading or mini-lessons, while small groups should include working at the students' instructional levels. Whole groups can take place at a gathering place for a brain and body break (Boushey & Moser, 2006). Independent groups may include work stations, computer work, independent reading,

Whole Group > Small Group > Whole Group > Small Group

4. **Schedule small group rotation instruction every day.** Guided Reading at the students' instructional reading level is still critical. Dr. Richard Allington has shared this message consistently and with seriousness over the years: "Research has well demonstrated the need for students to have instructional texts that they can read accurately, fluently, and with good comprehension if we hope to foster academic achievement." He has also reminded us, "Kids need to read a lot if they are to become good readers" (Allington) and to those of us who have listened to Dr. Allington speak, he is a strong supporter of texts kids can actually read, and leveled text fits that description. Share the purpose for the small-group lesson with your students. Always implement "before reading," "during reading," and "after reading" strategies with your students.

Looks Like:
- Reading is done by students
- Uses new, unseen text
- The teacher diagnoses, instructs, and evaluates during a small group reading lesson
- As each student simultaneously reads independently from his/her own copy of the text, the teacher observes behaviors, skills, and strategies – offering support as needed
- Is done in flexible groups that reflect the changing needs and abilities of students
- May have 3-6 groups
- K-2 small-groups may last 10-20 minutes
- 3-6 small groups may last 20-30 minutes
- Struggling readers should meet every day; All other students at least 2-4 times weekly.

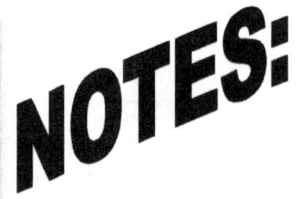

Selecting Leveled Text:
- Instructional reading level
- Reader's present strategies/interest/background knowledge
- Text complexity
- Appropriateness to age group
- Diversity represented
- Teachers' assessment of text and what students need to learn
- Quality of text, language, illustrations, layout, and writing
(Adapted from Benchmark Education Company)

Management of groups:
- Keep the rotation on a pie chart, using a clothes pin or clip for the groups or try pocket charts with students names/pictures and pictures of the stations.
- Use chimes or bell or some other cue for "time to move."
- Meeting for 15 minutes in the designated area (mine is on the floor) with your cue (chimes or "meet me in the hut") for whole group provides time for a mini lesson with the total group. Then, 15 minutes for a small group with you, and individual or small groups at work stations or around the room (their choice). Next 15 minutes whole group, and so on. Tip – if it's not working, you may start with 10-minute rotations and then increase the time as your students "get it" and know what to do during the independent time.
- Use a clipboard with a spreadsheet for informal assessment in a check-off format.

> Teacher meets with small group. Time is used to listen to students read, observe the students' use of strategues, provide assistance as needed, informally assess.

> Students are at work stations, or reading to self, reading to someone, listening to reading, writing, word work, or choosing to work on strategy for reinformcement. They are working either independently, with partners, or in triads.

> Students are at work stations, or reading to self, reading to someone, listening to reading, writing, word work, or choosing to work on strategy for reinformcement. They are working either independently, with partners, or in triads.

5. **Think about** how your teaching will look in both whole-group and small-group settings.

	K – 2
Whole-Group Teaching	• Interactive Read-Aloud • Shared/Choral Reading • Poetry Share and Mini Lesson • Readers' Theater • Phonics Mini-Lessons • Word Study Mini-Lessons • Interactive Vocabulary • Word Study Mini-Lessons • Reading Strategy Mini-lessons
Small-Group Teaching	• Guided Reading • Literature Study (Book Club) • Strategy Mini-Lessons
Individual Teaching	• Independent Reading • Buddy Reading • Reading Conferences • Diagnostic Assessments

(Adapted from Benchmark Education Company)

6. **Provide high quality independent work opportunities** for your students. Work Stations can be very effective in managing it all. Work Stations are used in short intervals and can include computer time

and/or independent or group strategy practice. You may also want to use a daily framework during that time - reading to self, reading to someone, listen to reading, work on writing, and word work; while also teaching students how to choose a "good fit book" as Allington refers to it *(Boushey and Moser, 2006, The Daily Five)*.

*"Daily Five builds on independent quality
literacy strategies, enabling me to do small groups.
Students love the choice factor.
You can implement it right away on day one or day fifty;
it doesn't matter. And charting in front of the students
[anchor charts], with the students' input, instead of
teacher charts becoming wallpaper, is so helpful.
We don't waste any time in my class –
there are precious important learning times
in my classroom and I want to keep them learning.
I absolutely love, love, love the concept of the Daily Five!"*
Ms. Jennifer Lahti, (Grades K, 1, and 2)
Mukilteo School District, Washington

7. **Use Anchor Charts to anchor the new learning to past learning, providing those connections** that are critical to student learning. Write them together with your students, using their ideas with yours, so they will feel ownership and pride. Use anchor charts for that important information you want your students to apply when working in small groups or on their own. Anchor charts should have a single focus, use student-friendly language written with them, and serve to anchor current understandings to future learning.

   Ways to store or share Anchor Charts:
   - Use chart stands
   - Hang from wall
   - Hang from ceiling
   - Attach to book shelves or other furniture
   - Type up each anchor chart and organize the printed copy in a binder for easy reference for you and your students; or
   - Take a picture of each anchor chart and scan to keep a record or use iPhoto or similar program. Then organize the printed copy in a binder for easy reference for you and your students.
   - Practice utilizing the Anchor Charts so your students will know your expectations and exactly how and when to use them.

8. **Look at your classroom with outside eyes** – is it an attractive place? It is a classroom you are proud to have set up? In my visitations to schools, teachers have shared that loving the space they are in helps them feel like they can manage it all. The following are examples of things I've seen in classrooms:
   a. A welcoming view from the doorway.
   b. Lamps – lots of lamps! One teacher didn't use the florescent overhead lighting – all lighting was provided by lamps and two windows. It added a very homey, comforting look to the classroom.
   c. Reading centers may include couches, rocking chairs, bean bag chairs, accent area rug, kid-size chairs. Small inner tubes, wading pool, sand chairs are often on sale at the end of the summer in some communities!
   d. Lots of books – in shelves, in baskets, in colorful buckets; displayed with front covers, by genre, leveled, by author, by topic, in individual student colorful boxes, in colorful plastic laundry bin (great for big books) – but easily accessible to all students. (Be ready for some incredible classroom pictures at our seminar!)
   e. Literacy workstations for centers – listening, writing, reading, recording, illustrations.
   f. Clearly defined spaces – work, floor, reading/classroom library, small group instruction area, whole group instruction area, labeled drawers/bins/baskets.
   g. Tub of clipboards for teachers and students.
   h. Whole group floor space or open area for chairs, writing easel/chart paper/dry erase/interactive type board, anchor charts.
   i. Small group area with table, chairs, place for materials, tubs/bins/baskets/shelves, chart paper/board/individual dry erase boards, anchor charts.
   j. One classroom in Tennessee had a dinette table and four chairs as the reading table, with a low/small vase of flowers and a tablecloth on it, all purchased from a yard sale/Craig's List. There was such a sense of pride and community in that classroom.
   k. Student desks grouped together for collaborative work – the message you are sending is "we work together." Colorful plastic cups/bins/baskets for

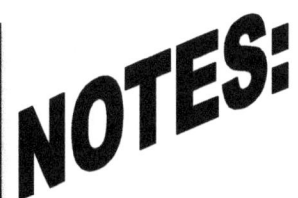

pencils, markers, crayons, wikki stix, highlighting tape.
l. iPod or CD player for instrumental music.
m. Art/creative area with scraps of paper, markers, crayons, book making materials, blue painter's tape. (nice if near the Writing station).
n. Felt with Velcro backing for word walls and displaying small anchor charts that can be taken on/off the wall for interactive strategy work.
o. Pillows, accent area rugs (not just for the reading center!)
p. Everything has a home.
q. Curtains – to cover some shelves that look "too busy," for windows, for door windows.
r. Planned color – keeping it to 2 or 3 colors is best. One teacher had all "accents" in a teal color – pillows, canvas bins, basket covers, accent rugs with teal as one of the colors, because she said it was her favorite color and it was very calming.
s. Word walls and ABC charts should be low enough where students can touch them. Not up high above the chalkboard or up high on a bulletin board – put ABC charts under the chalkboard or on student desks and in a workstation!
t. Places in the classroom where students can do partner reading, work together in partners or triads, can be floor space with area rugs or choices of stools/chairs. Overhead projector can be used on floor near wall or easel for partners/triads.
u. Student work displayed.
v. Plants, rugs, defined spaces, color-coordinated bins/baskets, shelves – are a necessity in some classrooms.

What would you add to this list? You are the experts in your classroom. What works for you?

"The common core standards
finally make real the promise of
American public education
to expect the best of all our schoolchildren."
Michael Casserly, Executive Director
Council of the Great City Schools

VI. Accelerate Reading Through the Gradual Release of Responsibility Model

NOTES:

Focus Lesson Teacher Demonstrates and Models "I do it"	Guided Instruction Guided Practice "We do it"	Collaborative "You do it together"	Independent I'm here to help as needed "You do it alone"
Teacher	Teacher	Teacher	Teacher
			STUDENT
		STUDENT	
	STUDENT		

Originally developed by David Pearson & Gallagher in 1983, with continued work from Doug Fisher and Nancy Frey, (2008) Regie Routman (2003) and Linda Dorn and Carla Soffos (2005), Benchmark Education, and others, show high quality teaching with the focus on developing independent learners. However, it is critical that all four steps are in place, and that we don't go straight to the "You do it" after a brief summary of what "you" are supposed to do.

© Gudwin, D. www.denise.gudwin.org

- "I do it"   Focus Lesson:
  Teachers Demonstrate and Model their own metacognitive practices as an active reader, using think alouds.

- "We do it"   Guided Instruction:
  Teachers prompt, question, and guide students through the practice, working together to obtain the desired goal.

- "You do it together"   Collaborative Learning
  Students work together to explore, make connections, transfer knowledge, discuss, problem solve, and work it out.

- "You do it"   Independent Learning
  Students are provided practice time to apply skills learned and use the strategies on their own. This step, after the focus lesson, guided instruction, and collaborative learning, is what helps students become active learners.

Reflect
When do you use the Gradual Release of Responsibility Model in your teaching day?

How does this connect to the Common Core?

In an effective classroom, gradual release of responsibility is occurring throughout the lesson, the day, the week, the unit of instruction; in various ways with individuals, small groups of students, as well as during whole group instruction.

Another way to look at it, specifically during our reading block…

Gradual Release of Responsibility	What the Teacher Says	What the Student Does	Reading
Model, Think Aloud, Demonstrate, Discuss	"I do it."	Student Observes and Reflects	Whole Group Read Aloud, Whole Group Mini-Lessons
Share, Model, Think Aloud, Demonstrate, Discuss	"I do it; but you do it with me some of the time."	Student observes and participates.	Whole Group Shared Reading, Whole Group Mini-Lessons
Guide	"You do it."	Student does most of the "work" with Teacher guiding and observing.	Small Group Guided Reading, Small Group Mini-Lesson
Practice	"You do it. And I'll observe. If you need help, I am nearby, but try using the strategies on your own first."	"Student is applying strategies independently, making personal connections, using anchor charts, following the modeling and guidance of the teacher.	Independent Reading and Independent Workstations

Adapted from Pearson & Gallagher (1983), Fisher, D., & Frey, N., (2008) Routman, R., (2003), Dorn, L., & Soffos, C., (2005), and Benchmark Education (2009).

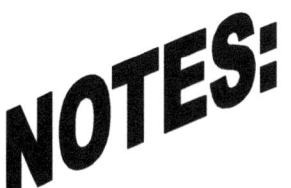

"Past Problems/Lessons Learned:
Too many standards, too little curriculum… And the textbook was the curriculum."
John Kendall, 2011

VII. Lessons Learned... How Do These Two Studies Connect to the Common Core Standards?

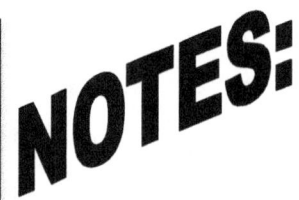

1) Ineffective Instructional Practice in First Grade

	Low Academic Quality	Mediocre Academic Quality	High Academic Quality
Positive Emotional Climate	31%	28%	23% were "top-notch"
Negative Emotional Climate	17%	-	-

Stulman, M.W. & Pianta, R. C. (2009). Profiles of educational quality in first grade. *Elementary School Journal, 109*(4), 323-342.

High academic ratings went to classrooms in which teachers (820 classrooms/32 states) engaged students in discussions, regularly provided students with constructive feedback on their work, and invited children to stretch their thinking.

**2) What Do Exemplary Teachers Look Like?
Learning to Read: Lessons from Exemplary First-Grade Classrooms.**

The authors wanted to know the difference between a great first-grade teacher and an exemplary first-grade teacher. They found that the exemplary teachers balanced all the "great teacher skills" such as "a commanding knowledge of classroom management; sound-, letter-, and word-level skills; children's literature; a variety of approaches to pedagogy (e.g., directing instruction, scaffolding, writers' workshop); and academic motivation." But in addition, the "excellent first-grade teacher combines these components every day, with expertise as impressive as that of a circus juggler riding a unicycle on a high wire without a net below. We're talking about 'complex instruction.' "

One of the connecting threads in all of the exemplary teachers' classrooms that they observed were two consistent instructional practices: 1) meaningful talk/conversations /discussions were ongoing, and 2) personalized instruction –

the exemplary teachers took into account the interests of the students, looking at the whole child, and personalized instruction to fit the needs of the students. This has a direct effect not only on comprehension, but also on motivation, interest, and stamina needed for successfully increasing achievement levels. Remember Charlie and the spider...

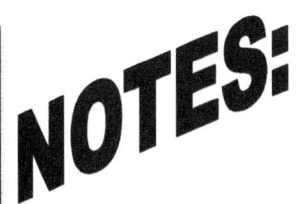

Pressley, M., Allington, R., Wharton-McDonald, R., Block, C., & Morrow, L.M. (2001). *Learning to Read: Lessons from Exemplary First-Grade Classrooms.* NY: Guilford Press.

Think of the grade level of your students...

- What connection can you make to this research of exemplary teachers?

- How does this apply to you?

Kindergarten Teacher

1st Grade Teacher

2nd Grade Teacher

3rd Grade or above Teacher

"Teachers who practice intentional instruction carefully select strategies appropriate to the type of content that students are learning and establish an environment conducive for learning by setting objectives, reinforcing effort, and providing recognition" (Dean, Hubbell, Pitler, & Stone, in press). Students are more likely to grasp a lesson objective that builds on their prior knowledge"
John Kendall, 2011

VIII. Additional Strategies

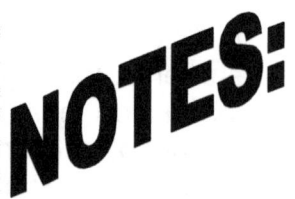

What do good readers do? Share with your readers what good readers do. Knowing what strategy to use when, will assist your students in becoming more effective readers. It shouldn't be a secret, yet when you ask struggling readers what good readers do, oftentimes they have no idea – the most common answer is, "They read fast." We must teach our students strategies that good readers use. See list shared at the seminar, and it can also be found on www.denise.gudwin.org. Create a list with your students, adding to it throughout the year.

1. _____
2. _____
3. _____
4. _____
5. _____
6. _____
7. _____
8. _____
9. _____
10. _____

Teaching Higher Order Thinking Through Think Alouds… Look back at "What Do Good Readers Do?" Good readers need to think while they are reading. By using modeling, coached practice, and reflection, you can teach your students strategies to help them think while they read and build their comprehension. (Farr, R., & Conner, J. www.readingrockets.org/article/102) Model this strategy by doing it yourself while trying to solve a reading problem such as finding an answer to a question, summarizing a paragraph, making meaning of a word…. Go through the think-aloud process with the students following along in their own text. Ask students to keep a list of the different things you do as you are trying to better understand the text. (Small groups of students work better than individually, in many cases.) You can turn these lists into anchor charts to help your students make these connections when they are applying strategies while reading on their own. Practice it on your own before you do it with your students! Teach your students to think aloud, share with a partner, expand on the think aloud, and then reflect. **When we model** the types of behaviors that good readers are engaged in, we provide our students with the opportunity to become aware of the many strategies and monitoring behaviors that good readers use. Thinking aloud helps students use higher order thinking skills.

Literature Circles – "where small groups of students gather to discuss a piece of literature in depth. The discussion is guided by students' response to what they have read. You may hear talk about events and characters in the book, the author's craft, or personal experiences related to the story. Literature Circles provide a way for students to engage in critical thinking and reflection as they read, discuss, and respond to books. Collaboration is at the heart of this approach. Students reshape and add onto their understanding as they construct meaning with other readers. Finally, literature circles guide students to deeper understanding of what they read through structured discussion and extended written and artistic response."
Schlick Noe, K., & Johnson, N. (1999)

Literature Circles Are…	Literature Circles Are Not…
Reader response centered	Teacher and text centered
Part of a balanced literacy program	The entire reading curriculum
Groups formed by book choice	Teacher-assigned groups formed solely by ability
Structured for student independence, responsibility, and ownership	Unstructured, uncontrolled 'talk time' without accountability
Guided primarily by student insights and questions	Guided primarily by teacher- or curriculum-based questions
Intended as a context in which to apply reading and writing skills	Intended as a place to do skills work
Flexible and fluid; never look the same twice	Tied to a prescriptive 'recipe'

Schlick Noe, K., & Johnson, N. (1999)

Mentor Texts… What are they and why do we use them?
Mentor texts or anchor texts are those really good books that we can use as examples for good writing. They also deserve credit under the category of "best books to read" because they expose our students to vocabulary, story grammar, think alouds, connections, background knowledge, sentence structure, character analysis, plot analysis, fluency practice, and tons more.

An example of sample mentor texts from http://nlu.nl.edu/rrconf/handouts/MaynardStratman-Genre-Studies.pdf might be helpful for us, as we start to explore the complexity, quality, and range of available books for our students -

Personal Narrative
- A Chair for My Mother
- When I Was Young in the Mountains

Narrative Story
- The Recess Queen
- Amazing Grace

Realistic Fiction
- The Night Tree
- My Rotten Red Headed Older Brother

Functional: Letters
- Dear Mrs. LaRue
- I Wanna Iguana

Expository: How To/Recipe
- How to Lose All Your Friends
- Pancakes for Breakfast

TIP: It would be most helpful if grade levels have a scheduled book talk a few times a month, and look at children's books in a more thoughtful "Core Standards" way.

Local libraries have various lists of books – here's one: *100 Books Every Child Should Hear Before Starting School*, Thanks to the King County Library System, Washington. What if our Kindergarteners, first graders, or second graders come to us not having heard most of these books (or any others)? We need to read aloud to our students. Every day. Just like we eat. And just like we need gas in our car (or a plug in for our electric car) to drive it, our students need to hear good books, for reading **and** writing **and** background

knowledge **and** vocabulary – **and** just for the love of reading…

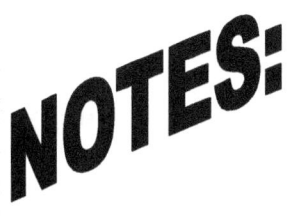

Recommended for Babies:
1. Ten, Nine, Eight by Mollly Bang
2. Goodnight Moon, by Margaret Wise Brown
3. The Very Hungry Caterpillar, by Eric Carle
4. Freight Train, by Donald Crews
5. Lunch, by Denise Fleming
6. Where's Spot, by Eric Hill
7. Is it Red? Is it Yellow? Is it Blue? An Adventure in Color, by Tana Hoban
8. Brown Bear, Brown Bear, by Bill Martin
9. Chicka, Chicka, Boom, Boom, by Bill Martin
10. Who's Counting? by Nancy Tafuri
11. How Do I Put It On? by Shigeo Watanabe

Recommended for Toddlers:
12. On The Day I Was Born, by Debbi Chocolate
13. Good Dog, Carl, by Alexandra Day
14. Feathers for Lunch, by Lois Ehlert
15. Go Away, Big Green Monster! by Ed Emberley
16. Ask Mr. Bear, by Marjorie Flack
17. Is Your Mama a Llama? by Deborah Guarina
18. Hush! A Thai Lullaby, by Minfong Ho
19. Rosie's Walk, by Pat Hutchins
20. Harold and the Purple Crayon, by Crockett Johnson
21. Jump, Frog, Jump! by Robert Kalan
22. The Teddy Bears' Picnic, by Jimmy Kennedy
23. Whose Mouse are You? by Robert Kraus
24. The Carrot Seed, by Ruth Krauss
25. Over in the Meadow, by John Langstaff
26. Dim Sum for Everyone! by Grace Lin
27. Little Blue and Little Yellow, by Leo Lionni
28. Guess How Much I Love You, by Sam McBratney
29. Whose Hat? by Margaret Miller
30. Shades of Black, by Sandra Pinkney
31. The Little Engine that Could, by Watty Piper
32. Good Night, Gorilla, by Peggy Rathmann
33. We're Going on a Bear Hunt, by Michael Rosen
34. Cars and Trucks and Things that Go, by Richard Scarry
35. Lizard's Song, by George Shannon
36. It Looked Like Spilt Milk, by Charles Shaw
37. Farmer Duck, by Martin Waddell

38. Mouse Paint, by Ellen Stoll Walsh
39. "Hi, Pizza Man!" by Virginia Walter
40. Noisy Nora, by Rosemary Wells
41. The Lady with the Alligator Purse, by Nadine Westcott
42. Buzz, by Janet Wong
43. The Napping House, by Audrey Wood

Recommended for Preschoolers:
44. Happy Birthday, Moon, by Frank Asch
45. Animals Should Definitely Not Wear Clothing, by Judi Barrett
46. Madeline, by Ludwig Bemelmans
47. The Mitten, by Jan Brett
48. Stone Soup, by Marcia Brown
49. The Story of Babar, the Little Elephant, by Jean de Brunhoff
50. Mr. Grumpy's Outing, by John Burningham
51. Mike Mulligan and His Steam Shovel, by Virginia Lee Burton
52. Mama Zooms, by Jane Cowen-Fletcher
53. The Empty Pot, by Demi
54. Pancakes for Breakfast, by Tomie DePaola
55. Abuela, by Authur Dorros
56. Are You My Mother? by P.D. Eastman
57. Corduroy, by Don Freeman
58. Millions of Cats, by Wanda Gag
59. The Three Billy Goats Gruff, by Paul Galdone
60. The Girl Who Loved Wild Horses, by Paul Goble
61. All the Colors of the Earth, by Sheila Hamanaka
62. Lilly's Puple Plastic Purse, by Kevin Henkes
63. Bread and Jam for Frances, by Russell Hoban
64. Amazing Grace, by Mary Hoffman
65. Angelina Ballerina, by Katherine Holabird
66. The Wolf's Chicken Stew, by Keiko Kasza
67. The Snowy Day, by Ezra Jack Keats
68. The Caterpillar and the Polliwog, by Jack Kent
69. Anansi and the Moss Covered Rock, by Eric Kimmel
70. I Took My Frogs to the Library, by Eric Kimmel
71. Tacky the Penguin, by Helen Lester
72. I Love You Like Crazy Cakes, by Rose Lewis
73. On Market Street, by Anita Lobel
74. Frog and Toad Are Friends, by Arnold Lobel
75. Frog Goes to Dinner, by Mercer Mayer

NOTES:

76. Make Way for Ducklings, by Robert McCloskey
77. Raven, by Gerald McDermott
78. Goin' Someplace Special, by Pat McKissack
79. Pigs Aplenty, Pigs Galore, by David McPhail
80. Martha Speaks, by Susan Meddaugh
81. The Day Jimmy's Boa Ate the Wash, by Trinka Noble
82. If You Give a Mouse a Cookie, by Laura Numeroff
83. The Ant and the Elephant, by Bill Peet
84. The Talk of Peter Rabbit, by Beatrix Potter
85. Martin's Big Words: The Life of Martin Luther King, Jr., by Doreen Rappaport
86. Curious George, by H. A. Rey
87. The Relatives Came, by Cynthia Rylant
88. Grandfather's Journey, by Allen Say
89. Where the Wild Things Are, by Maurice Sendak
90. The Cat in the Hat, by Dr. Seuss
91. Caps for Sale, by Esphyr Slobodkina
92. Imogene's Antlers, by David Small
93. Snapshots from the Wedding, by Gary Soto
94. Sylvester and the Magic Pebble, by William Steig
95. There Was an Old Lady Who Swallowed a Fly, by Simms Taback
96. Alexander and the Terrible, Horrible, No Good, Very Bad Day, by Judith Viorst
97. Lyle, Lyle Crocodile, by Bernard Waber
98. Owl Moon, by Jane Yolen
99. Seven Blind Mice, by Ed Young
100. Harry, the Dirty Dog, by Gene Zion

Add Your Favorites:

Reading Standards for Literature K-5

Reading Standards for Literature

Reading Standards for Literature holds the core of most of the reading strategies you are currently teaching. The Common Core Standards "kick it up a notch" and include more rigorous teaching and learning opportunities.

Reading Standards for Literature		
Kindergarten Students	**Grade 1 Students**	**Grade 2 Students**
RL.K.2 With prompting and support, retell familiar stories, including key details.	**RL.1.2** Retell stories, including key details, and demonstrate understanding of their central message or lesson.	**RL.2.2** Recount stories, including fables and folktales from diverse cultures, and determine their central message, lesson, or moral.
RL.K.7 With prompting and support, describe the relationship between illustrations and the story in which they appear (e.g., what moment in a story an illustration depicts).	**RL.1.7** Use illustrations and details in a story to describe its characters, setting, or events.	**RL.2.7** Use information gained from the illustrations and words in a print or digital text to demonstrate understanding of its characters, setting, or plot.
Strategies: The following 5 strategies provide opportunities for effective teaching and learning.		

Read and Retell is a strategy that is very powerful. The original research was conducted by Brown and Cambourne. Check out the retelling graphic organizers in the Appendix.

- **Oral Retelling** Encourage the students to retell the story, page-by-page, while first looking at the pictures. Later, encourage them to retell without seeing the illustrations. You may want to use the retelling glove (seen today) for a visual cue. The steps are the same as the Written retelling, with the exception of the writing. Another option is to retell through pictures or drawing.

- **Written Retelling**
  1) Read a passage
  2) (Addition to the original steps – discuss with someone before writing)

3) Written Retell
4) Share retelling with a partner (Pair-Share)
   a. *Pair Share*: Share with your partner. Take turns.
   b. *Borrowed Bits*: Did your partner say something that you liked? You can borrow something from your partner and add it to your own writing.
   c. *Muddled Meanings:* Was there something you said or wrote that didn't make sense to your partner? Clarify it, say it, or write it a different way.
5) Revise your retelling; make it better. Use a special writing pen.

Speaking and Writing, Vocabulary and Listening:
- *Linguistic Spillover* is a phenomenon that occurs as children begin to use the *language of the author* in their written retells. This occurs in children as young as pre-kindergarten.

Retelling – Real Teachers Share
- "After predicting and thinking of words that might be in the article, I could tell their excitement to read the article was building. They loved making predictions on sticky notes."
- "Michael usually never writes a lot and for this retell, he wrote the most."
- LESSONS LEARNED: "I did what was advised. I read the students' last retells to the entire class – what an experience; they were all beaming with pride. I ensured to make at least two positive comments about retelling components (using quotes or sequencing or recalling details) and this week I noticed that the students attitudes toward retelling have changed."
- "To hear the kids speak about it (oral retellings) to hear them and their expressions, 'and the lion will swallow me…' it is incredible. Because the oral language is without mistakes, you can't see the spelling errors and the handwriting. The big point is they get to say it without me concentrating on the mechanics. They were so into it."
- "I asked them how they felt about this assignment. One student, Javier, said, 'I felt like I was the author.' "
- "As we were reading, Paulo said, 'You won't believe me, but all of the words I put for the prediction are in here.' I thought that was pretty neat. He got very excited."
- "One of the students said, 'I would do a retell before that reading workbook any day!' I found that very interesting because I rarely use the reading workbook."

Gudwin (2002) ERIC Document ED466869

Making Connections: Text-to-self, text-to-text, and text-to-world is a strategy that brings understanding to our students. Model by showing the connections you make in a think aloud. Keene and Zimmerman (1997) conducted research on making connections when reading. They concluded that students comprehend better when they make connections such as 1) text-to-self, 2) text-to-text, and 3) text-to-world. An example of text-to-self might be, *"This story reminds me of when I went ice skating with my grandpa."* The reader brings in background knowledge and connects to the text in oftentimes an emotional sense. Text-to-text: *"This character reminds me of the character in the story we read last week. They are both very stubborn."* A text-to-world connection may be, *"That reminds me of the Discovery channel – I saw a program about that this past summer."* Part of what the reader is doing is forming a picture in their head while reading and understanding it better. (Tovani, 2000) Make a connection with Background Knowledge – Critical!

Character Analysis helps children connect with the character and understand others' points of view.

Compare and Contrast using a new hands-on approach will help your students be more successful in applying this strategy.

Background Knowledge
I believe this to be one of the most powerful pieces of the comprehension puzzle. Tune in to the background knowledge activity during this session for an ah-ha moment.

Some of My Favorite Children's Books for Standards RL.K.2, RL.1.2, RL.2.2 RL.K.7, RL.1.7, and RL.2.7
Listen to the Rain   By Bill Martin Jr. and John Archambault, Illustrated by James Endicott
Llama Llama Red Pajama   By Anna Dewdney
The Seashore Book   By Charlotte Zolotow, Paintings by Wendell Minor
Dear Max   By Sally Grindley, Illustrated by Tony Ross

Reading Standards for Informational Text K-5

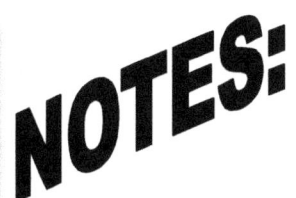

Informational Text provides one of the keys to success in later schooling and it prepares our students for real-life reading. Many of our children prefer informational text because it focuses on interests and answers questions that children have. "Informational Texts may be particularly well-suited to contributing to young children's development of vocabulary and world knowledge" (Duke, N. 2003).

Reading Standards for Informational Text		
Kindergarten Students	**Grade 1 Students**	**Grade 2 Students**
RI.K.5 Identify the front cover, back cover, and title page of a book.	RI.1.5 Know and use various text features (e.g., headings, tables of contents, glossaries, electronic menus, icons) to locate key facts or information in a text.	RI.2.5 Know and use various text features (e.g., captions, bold print, subheadings, glossaries, indexes, electronic menus, icons) to locate key facts or information in a text efficiently.
RI.K.6 Name the author and illustrator of a text and define the role of each in presenting the ideas or information in a text.	RI.1.6 Distinguish between information provided by pictures or other illustrations and information provided by the words in a text.	RI.2.6 Identify the main purpose of a text, including what the author wants to answer, explain, or describe.
The following six effective strategies will engage your students in non-fiction, informational text.		

Strategies

3-2-1 is a great strategy for children. Model it many times first, using the Gradual Release of Responsibility. 3 things you discovered, 2 things you found interesting, and 1 question you still have. (Zygouris-Coe, V., Wiggins, M, & Smith, L. 2004). It can be adapted to fit the needs of your students.

Book Walk/Book Talk or Picture Walk/Picture Talk: A great strategy that can be accomplished individually or in small groups. The student needs to see the book while the teacher talks about it, page-by-page. The teacher turns the pages of the book, one-by-one, and describes what is in the pictures, the captions, the sidebars, the bold print, all the text features that are crucial to the meaning of the text. Remember my student Abraham, "I'm not scared about reading anymore?" This is one of two strategies (beginning with Picture Walk/Picture talk – when you only look at the pictures and talk about what the illustrations are telling you) that opened the door of reading for Abraham.

Genre Study exposes children to the various types of reading that is available to them. The central goals are to support students in reading, comprehending, and analyzing genres. Common nonfiction genres include Biography, Book Review, Informational Text, Journals, Memoirs, Personal Narratives, and Persuasive Letters/Essays (Benchmark Education). Reading in the Genre should include comprehension strategies, vocabulary, analysis of the way the genre is designed, response to text, text-to-text connections, and fluency. IRA/NCTE have provided a genre study book list that might be of interest to you (www.readwrite think.org/files/resource/lesson_images /lesson270/genre_books.pdf). The categories are Realistic Fiction, Historical Fiction, Fantasy/Science Fiction, and Mystery. However, they are not leveled, but may be used for read alouds or shared reading.

6-Point Storyboard is an option for students to use with a variety of assignments. It is a simple graphic organizer that can hone in on various strategies. Try this for many different types of assignments. Add any question/topic/concept in the boxes. See sample shared today.

Self-Monitoring Text – Janet Allen's work, as well as others, supports this strategy for readers.
Do I…
- ☑ Know when I don't get it?
- ☑ Use strategies?
- ☑ Know which strategies to use?
- ☑ Keep information organized (sticky notes)
- ☑ Write, highlight, & draw pictures to help me remember?
- ☑ Know what confuses me and ask for help?
- ☑ Pay attention to heading, bold print?
- ☑ Notice the way the page is set up?
- ☑ Read the captions that go with the pictures?

Metacognitive Strategies: Using Anchor Charts, flip books, and bookmarks as effective teaching tools, teach, model, and practice the use of metacognitive strategies. Always share the purpose with your students, the why and how this will help you. Benchmark Education (www.benchmarkeducation. com) includes the following Metacognitive Strategies (among others) in their Assessment Checklist for Metacognitive and Comprehension Strategy Development – here is a sampling:

Determine Text Importance
- I know these parts of the story are important because…
- I need to pay attention to this _____ . It has information I need.
- I think the author thought _____ is important because…

Ask Questions
- What does the word _____ mean on this page?
- Why is the author giving me so much information about…?
- What would I do if I were in the same situation as [a character]?

Fix Up Monitoring
- I didn't understand that. Maybe I should reread it more slowly.
- Wait a minute. I need to stop and think.
- The author says _____. What does that mean?

Make Connections
- This reminds of when I … (Text to Self)
- This character is just like the character in… (Text to Text)
- If this character were alive today, I bet she would be… (Text to World)

Make Inferences
- The author says _____. I think she means…
- If I read between the lines, the author is telling me…
- These few pieces of evidence [clues] tell me that…

Some of My Favorite Children's Books for Standards RI.K.5, RI.1.5, and RI.2.5
What Color is Nature? By Stepen R. Swinburne
Chameleon, Chamelion By Joy Cowley, Photographs by Nic Bishop
Non Fiction Nature Treasure: A First Look at the Natural World By Lizann Flatt
Throw Your Tooth on the Roof: Tooth Traditions From Around the World By Selby Beeler
Picasso and Minou By P. I. Maltbie, Illustrated by Pau Estrada

Reading Standards: Foundational Skills

Phonics and Word Recognition/Word Work for those students needing the foundational skills in reading includes some of the following phonics-based activities:

Reading Standards: Foundational Skills #3		
Kindergarten Students	**Grade 1 Students**	**Grade 2 Students**
FS.K.3 Know and apply grade-level phonics and word analysis skills in decoding words. a. Demonstrate basic knowledge of one-to-one letter-sound correspondences by producing the primary or many of the most frequent sound for each consonant. b. Associate the long and short sounds with common spellings (graphemes) for the five major vowels. c. Read common high-frequency words by sight (e.g., *the, of, to, you, she, my, is, are, do, does*). d. Distinguish between similarly spelled words by identifying the sounds of the letters that differ.	**FS.1.3** Know and apply grade-level phonics and word analysis skills in decoding words. a. Know the spelling-sound correspondences for common consonant digraphs. b. Decode regularly spelled one-syllable words. c. Know final –e and common vowel team conventions for representing long vowel sounds. d. Use knowledge that every syllable must have a vowel sound to determine the number of syllables in a printed word. e. Decode two-syllable words following basic patterns by breaking the words into syllables. f. Read words with inflectional endings. g. Recognize and read grade-appropriate irregularly spelled words.	**FS.2.3** Know and apply grade-level phonics and word analysis skills in decoding words. a. Distinguish long and short vowels when reading regularly spelled one-syllable words. b. Know spelling-sound correspondences for additional common vowel teams. c. Decode regularly spelled two-syllable words with long vowels. d. Decode words with common prefixes and suffixes. e. Identify words with inconsistent but common spelling-sound correspondences. f. Recognize and read grade-appropriate irregularly spelled words.
Strategies: The following five strategies will provide worthwhile practice in word work. They can be adapted for any grade level to fit the needs of your learners.		

© Gudwin, D. www.denise.gudwin.org

Strategies

Onset and Rime: Teaching your students the 37 basic rimes (spelling patterns) assist children in reading and spelling over 500 primary level words (Cunningham, 2000). Utilize the list in the Appendix!

Guess the Covered Word helps children "learn that just guessing words is not a good decoding strategy, but when they guess something that makes sense in the sentence, has all the right letters up to the vowel (not just the first one), and is the right length, they can figure out many new words" (Cunningham, 2009, p.56). Guess the Covered Word is an effective strategy that encourages students to use context and letter-sound information to figure out words in a fill-in-the-blank sentence. Write 1 – 4 sentences with a key word covered in each sentence. Use two sticky notes to cover, the first one covering the rime portion, and the second one covering the onset portion of the word. Read the first sentence together: My favorite pet is a _____. Students make a guess for the word represented by the line, using context clues. Appropriate guesses may be dog, cat, iguana, bird, turtle... Then, remove one of the sticky notes underneath, and students will see, My favorite pet is a p_____. Now, the student's guess will start to tune into the letter-sound information. Guesses may include puppy or pig. When you remove the second sticky note, you will show the word in its entirety. My favorite pet is a parrot. Model sounding out the word in syllables.

Be a Mind Reader
A flexible and effective strategy (Cunningham, 2009) for reinforcing phonics strategies previously taught. You create the clues, and they can (and should) be different for each group. Tailor it to the needs of your students. This is appropriate for any grade level. Example Activity:

1. _____
2. _____
3. _____
4. _____
5. _____

Sorting Word Cards Into Patterns and Transfer: Use your word wall cards or your "Making Words" cards to guide students into sorting words by patterns. Model how you focus on the onset and rime patterns, the vowel patterns, or the prefix/suffix patterns. During reading and writing, encourage your students to use the Anchor Charts or Word Walls to apply knowledge learned.

Rounding Up the Rhymes is an activity you can use with any read-aloud, leveled book, or shared reading book that you are using in a lesson. You reread the story, and have your children help you "round up the rhymes" (Cunningham, 2009) by deciding which words on the page are rhyming words. Use highlighter, wikki stix, highlighting tape, pointer, finger, tracker, or write them down! Use both oral and written responses combined.

Some of My Favorite Children's Book for Standards FS.K.3, FS.1.3, FS.2.3
My Big Dog   By Janet Stevens and Susan Stevens Crummel   *The Library*   Sarah Stewart, Illustrated by David Small   *More Parts*   By Ted Arnold   *Mousetrap*   By Diane Snowball, Illustrated by Kathi Ember

Reading Standards: Foundational Skills

Owning the Strategies of a Fluent Reader: Fluent readers are better readers (Moss and Young, 2010) – and you will hopefully have another "ah-ha" moment at the seminar regarding fluency. "The fluent reader is one who can perform multiple tasks – such as word recognition and comprehension – at the same time. The nonfluent reader, on the other hand, can perform only one task at any time" (National Reading Panel, 2000). "Even with adequate comprehension, slow and labored reading will turn any school or recreational reading assignment into a marathon of frustration for nearly any student." (Rasinski, 2003). Rasinki says "Sing with your kids; singing is a wonderful way to increase fluency" (2010). If you find a Karaoke machine at a yard sale, pick it up for your classroom!

What do you do to build fluency besides a word correct per minute probe (wcpm)?

Reading Standards: Foundational Skills #4		
Kindergarten Students	**Grade 1 Students**	**Grade 2 Students**
FS.K.4 Read emergent-reader texts with purpose and understanding.	FS.1.4 Read with sufficient accuracy and fluency to support comprehension. a. Read on-level text with purpose and understanding b. Read on-level text orally with accuracy, appropriate rate, and expression on successive readings. c. Use context to confirm or self-correct word recognition and understanding, rereading as necessary.	FS.2.4 Read with sufficient accuracy and fluency to support comprehension. a. Read on-level text with purpose and understanding b. Read on-level text orally with accuracy, appropriate rate, and expression on successive readings. c. Use context to confirm or self-correct word recognition and understanding, rereading as necessary.
Strategies: The following three strategies will provide students a variety of ways to practice fluency in a meaningful way.		

Strategies

Fluency Cards: You will see how a simple sentence can turn into a great activity for your students, with the rigor of grade-level text and the challenge to apply the strategy when reading independently. Write the same sentence of four different cards. Group your students to read the same sentence aloud four different ways: 1) angry, 2) excited, 3) scared, and 5) surprised. Discuss how the context clues in the story influence how the sentences are read. This strategy helps make the point of reading fluently with expression and how it helps with comprehension. We will demonstrate this at today's session – it's a keeper. Many teachers have tried it with their students and found it to be motivating and effective.

Fluency Chunk: The Fluency Chunk is a valuable strategy for struggling readers (Miami-Dade County Public Schools). If you only try one strategy from today (impossible!) this one is a keeper. It is easy to use and can be added to your already existing reading program.
1) Choose a grade-level passage/chunk. (Even if it is too difficult for them to read.)
2) Read the passage/chunk aloud to your students. (Read To)

© Gudwin, D. www.denise.gudwin.org

3) Then, read the same passage/chunk again, using choral reading with all students and you reading it together. (Read With)
4) Choose 3-5 target words from the same passage/chunk. Write them on the board or on word cards. The students visually match the word to the text, finding it in the passage/chunk. The students then chorally or individually read the whole sentence in which the word was found. Repeat with each of the target words.
5) Next, each student buddy-reads the same passage/chunk with a partner. (Read By) Each partner has a job – while one student is reading, the partner holds the marker and tracks the sentence. When the other student reads, the partner holds the marker and tracks the sentence. With this tracking activity, both students are actively involved in reading the passage.
6) Repeat any steps if needed. Often teachers decide to choral read or a read aloud again at the end.
7) The same passage/chunk, repeating steps 2-6, is read on Monday, Tuesday, Wednesday, Thursday, and Friday. By the end of the week, even your most struggling students think they can read it… and if they think they can, they can.
8) The same passage/chunk can be sent home for homework/home learning for repeated readings.

Can you see from the demonstration how the Fluency Chunk increases fluency, word recognition, new word identification, self-esteem, and motivation, especially if grade-level text is too difficult for them to read on their own? Try it! (Are any of you Reading Recovery Teachers? Does this sound familiar?) This strategy also demonstrates Gradual Release of Responsibility within the strategy.

Rereading – Ways to Bring Fun Into Fluency Practice. By using a variety of reading materials, sharing the purpose of rereading, and using color and body motions, you will find your students practicing fluency through rereading.
- Color code text – one group reads the blue, another group reads the red text
- Use ideas from children's books shared at the seminar
- Students can practice for a variety of purposes (read to the principal, read to another class, record voice memo on a smart phone)

Word-by-Word Reading: Included here to help you remember the demonstration at the seminar. Word-by-word reading so impacts our students' reading comprehension.

Some of My Favorite Children's Books for Standards FS.K.4, FS.1.4, and FS.2.4
I Am the Dog, I am the Cat By Donald Hall and Barry Moser *You Read to Me, I'll Read to you: Very Short Fairy Tales to Read Together* By Mary Ann Hoberman, Illustrated by Michael Emberley *You Read to Me, I'll Read to You: Very Short Stories to Read Together* By Mary Ann Hoberman, Illustrated by Michael Emberley *You Read to Me, I'll Read to you: Very Short Fables to Read Together* By Mary Ann Hoberman, Illustrated by Michael Emberley *You Read to Me, I'll Read to You* By John Ciardi, Illustrated by Edward Gorey

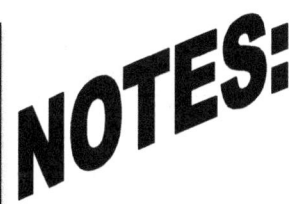

Speaking and Listening Standards K-5

*Note: We are focusing on **Reading Standards** in this seminar, however, because oral language/speaking and listening comprehension is so connected to reading, I have included strategies that are essential to the K-2nd grade teaching and learning experience.*

Comprehension and Collaboration: Oral Language is critical to the development of listening comprehension, reading comprehension, vocabulary development, and expressive/receptive language in general. Talk to your students. Listen to your students! To increase oral language, provide your students the opportunity for both social talk and academic talk. Turn and talk, elbow-elbow-knee-knee, eye-eye-knee-knee, talking partners… all are valuable ways to encourage talking, engage your students in the learning process, and increase oral language and comprehension.

Think back at Hart and Risley's research, as well as Pressley, Allington, Wharton-McDonald, Block, and Morrow's research.

Kindergarten Students	Grade 1 Students	Grade 2 Students
SL.K.1 1. Participate in collaborative conversations with diverse partners about *kindergarten topics and texts* with peers and adults in small and larger groups. a) Follow agreed-upon rules for discussions (e.g., listening to others and taking turns speaking about the topics and texts under discussion). b) Continue a conversation through multiple exchanges.	**SL.1.1** 1. Participate in collaborative conversations with diverse partners about *grade 1 topics and texts* with peers and adults in small and larger groups. a) Follow agreed-upon rules for discussions (e.g. listening to others with care, speaking one at a time about the topics and texts under discussion). b) Build on others' talk in conversations by responding to the comments of others through multiple exchanges. c) Ask questions to clear up any confusion about the topics and texts under discussion.	**SL.2.1** 1. Participate in collaborative conversations with diverse partners about *grade 2 topics and texts* with peers and adults in small and larger groups. a) Follow agreed-upon rules for discussions (e.g., gaining the floor in respectful ways, listening to others with care, speaking one at a time about the topics and texts under discussion.) b) Build on others' talk in conversations by linking their comments to the remarks of others. c) Ask for clarification and further explanation as needed about the topics and texts under discussion.

Strategies

The following strategies are effective for all grade levels, although it will look different in a kindergarten class than it does in a 2nd grade class, and will look different in one grade level/different classrooms! Think TEAM:

Together
Everyone
Achieves
More

NOTES:

Strategies

Engage your students in meaningful talk. This includes: partner chats, timed pair shares, inside outside circle, triad talk, cooperative groupings, where students have roles in their groups, small group discussions, large group discussions, book talks, strategy shares. Think back to the research of Pressley, Allington, et al., Kagan, and Hart & Risley for your rationale.

- Inside Outside Circle
    - Students are in partners, facing each other. Partner A on the inside, Partner B on the outside (You can also form a large circle, count off A, B. A's move to the outside, B's stay on the inside.)
    - Partner A shares a response to a question provided by the teacher with Partner B. Then Partner B shares his/her answer. Or, questions can be on two sets of cards (one for the inside circle and one for the outside circle) instead of the teacher asking them.
    - The outside circle (or the inside circle) rotates clockwise and with another partner, and another, shares their responses with new partners.
- Jigsaw
    - Choose a reading selection that has various pages/parts to it. (Can be pictures or text). Separate it into ___ sections. For this example, we will separate it into 4 sections. You will want to have the same number of sections as you have students in your group.
    - Pass out the reading/picture selection to the total group. Build background knowledge together.
    - Divide the students into home groups. If students are already sitting at tables, they can serve as the home group. If the reading/picture selection has four sections to it, you will need four home groups, with four students in each group. Each member of the home group will be responsible for a section.
    - Count off each student, 1-2-3-4. This will give you 4 expert groups. All of the 1s meet together, all of the 2s meet together, all of the 3s, and all of the 4s, forming four expert groups.
    - Set aside time for the four expert groups to read and discuss their selection. For example, the 1s meet together read/preview pictures of section one. The expert groups decide what are the most important parts of their section that they will share out to their home group. This cooperative expert group serves as guidance for the members of the group who need additional assistance.
    - Then the students in each of the expert groups go back to their home groups, and the "1" discusses the important parts of section one, the "2" discusses

the important parts of section two, and so on. Each person (the expert now) takes a turn sharing to the home group.
- Teacher may follow-up with total group oral discussion.
(Gudwin, 2008)

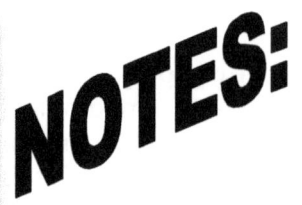

- Possible Roles for Cooperative Groups (Kagan)
  - Leader
  - Recorder
  - Spokesperson
  - Timekeeper
  - Summarizer
  - Reflector
  - Connector
  - Encourager
  - Praiser
  - Taskmaster
  - Checker
- Strategy Shares – Students describe how and when they use a particular strategy successfully. It can be as simple as using partners, triads, small groups or more complex using an Inside Outside Circle, Numbered Heads, (counting off 1-2-3-4 and all the fours get together and discuss, with one student sharing out), Four Corners, or even Jigsaw.
- Four Corners
  - Count students off 1-2-3-4.
  - All the 1s go to one corner of the room, the 2s go to another corner, the 3s go to a third corner of the room, and the 4s go to the last corner of the room.
  - Discussions can then be paired, triads, or small group discussions on a topic/question.

Collaborative Conversations among their peers is part of this standard and will need to be taught. (Tip: If your classroom is set up in collaborative groupings, you will already have an advantage in achieving this goal.)

- Students will need definite guidelines that include modeling "What This Looks Like" and "What This Sounds Like." (I would also include "What This DOESN'T Look Like" and What This DOESN'T Sound Like.")
- After you feel they understand their responsibility in this task, then engage them in a role-playing activity, first in small groups or partners, while you observe, listen, and guide them.
- When you have 4 or 5 students who are demonstrating an understanding of what to do, then engage them in a Fishbowl activity, where the fishbowl group is sitting in a circle and the rest of the class is sitting either in an outside circle or together outside of the inner circle.

- Rules: 1) The fishbowl group sits in the inside circle. 2) Observers (the rest of the students) sit in the outside circle. 3) Observers may not talk. Their job is to listen and reflect. 4) Everyone in the fishbowl group has an opportunity to talk.
- You may use this strategy in a 5-minute fishbowl or longer.
- After the fishbowl talk, facilitate a whole group discussion with the observing students and the fishbowl students.
- Encourage the fishbowl group to provide their own feedback at the end.

Some of My Favorite Children's Books for Standards SL.K.1, SL.1.1, and SL.2.1 *(Although ANY of the books listed for this seminar fit!)*
Tomorrow's Alphabet   By George Shannon and Donald Crews
Looking Closely Along the Shore   By Frank Serafini
Out of the Ocean   By Debra Frasier
Kites Sail High: A Book About Verbs   By Ruth Heller

Speaking and Listening Standards K-5

*Note: We are focusing on **Reading Standards** in this seminar, however, because oral language/speaking and listening comprehension is so connected to reading, I have included strategies that are essential to the K-2nd grade teaching and learning experience.*

As previously discussed, **Oral Language** is critical to the development of listening comprehension, reading comprehension, vocabulary development, and expressive/receptive language in general. Talk to your students. Listen to your students! To increase oral language, provide your students the opportunity for both social talk and academic talk. Turn and talk, elbow-elbow-knee-knee, eye-eye-knee-knee, talking partners… all are valuable ways to encourage talking, engage your students in the learning process, and increase oral language and comprehension. provide your students opportunities to describe and create stories orally; To increase oral language, provide your students opportunities to talk to each other and you, and to describe and create stories orally.

Speaking and Listening Standards K-5 Presentation of Knowledge and Ideas, #4		
Kindergarten Students	**Grade 1 Students**	**Grade 2 Students**
SL.K.4 Describe familiar people, places, things, and event and, with prompting and support, provide additional detail.	**SL.1.4** Describe people, places, things, and event with relevant details, expressing ideas and feelings clearly.	**SL.2.4** Tell a story or recount an experience with appropriate facts and relevant, descriptive details, speaking audibly in coherent sentences.
Strategies: The three strategies below will provide you with support on building oral language and literacy with your students.		

Strategies

Build a Story: A successful strategy providing children a structured opportunity to create an oral story, one sentence at a time, based on a picture or theme. The story builds on the previously stated sentence, so good listening skills and comprehension is important. The story may be written and reread at a later time. Sentences can be put on sentence strips and used for sequencing, also at a later time. Rereading familiar text is another great strategy that can be combined with this one as a follow-up.

Talk to your students! Hart and Risley (1995) in "Meaningful Differences in the Everyday Experience of Young American Children" projected from their research that children hear between 13 million and 45 million words by the time they are four years old. You and I both know that we can identify the children who have only been exposed to 13 million words, even during the first week of school! Let's tie that into learning to read...

Telling our story before hearing the author's story: Do a Picture Walk-Picture Talk first, looking at the pictures page by page. Then explain that we are going to tell our own story, based on the pictures from the book. Cover up the text with sticky notes, which can be used to write your group story. Encourage oral discussion focusing on the pictures, and write down what the students say for each page. The children become the author of the story, and their "new" story will probably become their favorite. Read the group story together each day, and if the students want to add to it, they can. This is an effective extension to a Language Experience Story. After numerous readings, you can read the "real author's" story, and compare the two, in another oral discussion. I have found this strategy to be particularly motivating to young students.

Some of My Favorite Children's Books for Standards SL.K.4, SL.1.4, and SL.2.4
The Little Mouse, the Red Ripe Strawberry, and the Big Hungry Bear By Audrey Woods and Don Woods ***Carl Goes to Daycare*** By Alexandra Day ***The Red Book*** By Barbara Lehman ***Chalk*** By Bill Thomson

Language Standards K-5

*Note: We are focusing on **Reading Standards** in this seminar, however, because Language Standards include vocabulary, which is so connected to reading, I have included strategies that are essential to the K-2nd grade teaching and learning experience.*

Vocabulary Acquisition and Use: Disadvantaged students in the first grade have a vocabulary that is approximately half that of an advantaged student, 2,900 and 5,800 respectively (readfaster.com). Some of our more current definitions of "disadvantaged" include diversity, economics, and even those who are not learning at the same rate. Vocabulary and background knowledge are main components of comprehension (Moss and Young, 2010, Soto-Hinman and Hetzel, 2009). Vocabulary/language are important components of reading, and are listed as Language Standards, Vocabulary Acquisition and Use, in the Common Core Standards.

How does vocabulary impact comprehension and writing?

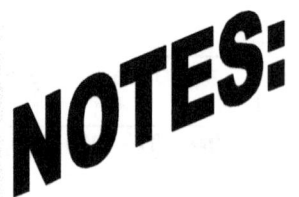

Language Standards K-5 Vocabulary Acquisition and Use #5		
Kindergarten Students	**Grade 1 Students**	**Grade 2 Students**
L.K.5a and L.K.5d With guidance and support from adults, explore word relationships and nuances in word meanings. a) Sort common objects into categories (e.g., shapes, foods) to gain a sense of the concepts the categories represent. d) Distinguish shades of meaning among verbs describing the same general action (e.g., *walk, march, strut, prance*) by acting out the meaning.	**L.1.5a and L.1.5d** With guidance and support from adults, demonstrate understanding of word relationships and nuances in word meanings. a) Sort words into categories (e.g., colors, clothing) to gain a sense of the concepts the categories represent. d) Distinguish shades of meaning among verbs differing in manner (e.g., *look, peek, glance, stare, glare, scowl*) and adjectives differing in intensity (e.g., *large, gigantic*) by defining or choosing them or by acting out the meanings.	**L.2.5a and L.2.5b** Demonstrate understanding of word relationships and nuances in word meanings. a) Identify real-life connections between words and their use (e.g., describe foods that are *spicy* or *juicy*). b) Distinguish shades of meaning among closely related verbs (e.g., *toss, throw, hurl*) and closely related adjectives (e.g., *thin, slender, skinny, scrawny*).
Strategies: The four strategies below will engage your students in the learning process of increasing vocabulary for the purpose of enjoying literacy. Given that the understanding of vocabulary also increases comprehension, strengthening their enjoyment of learning new vocabulary will help create better readers.		

Strategies

List – Group – Label is a vocabulary and comprehension strategy that helps build background knowledge, develop group or categorization skills, utilize higher order thinking skills, practice problem solving, and increase vocabulary. Model the strategy first. Then work together as a whole group and do it together. Small groups can practice the activity after you have modeled it, using the "I do" and the "We Do" in group practice. During modeling, think aloud on why you are putting the words in a certain group. Using this Gradual Release of Responsibility will ensure a higher rate of success. Share the purpose of using this strategy with your students, to help us use the words, to help us know the meaning of the words.

Step 1: Brainstorm a list of words related to a topic (Topic may be selected by the teacher). Visually display all of the words.

Step 2: Group the words, and cluster them into categories. Tell your students that there is no right or wrong answer, if they can explain why they feel a word goes in a particular group. Encourage your students to discuss the words and their thinking as to which group they go into.

Step 3: Label the groups with a descriptive title.

Sort and Describe is a vocabulary strategy that includes "doing" and "talking" in a way that engages all learners. (Adapted from a parent workshop with Page Ahead/Families Read. Seattle, Washington) Provide a variety of items for small groups of students to touch, smell, discuss. (i.e., rocks, stones - some shiny, some not, and in different shades of color, furry balls, pieces of wood, buttons of various shapes and colors) Items can be categorized, vocabulary lists can be created, and discussion of items should be encouraged. See sample at seminar.

Word Collections: What can we learn from "Donovan's Word Jar" or "Max's Words" when we apply this strategy to our classroom? Brainstorm words to go into a category. This time, you are providing the category title first. This activity, coupled with graphic organizers, (see appendix) helps build vocabulary and confidence, as well as the love of learning and using new words, which increases reading comprehension, and speaking, writing, and reading vocabulary.

Linear Arrays are a visual, hands-on representation of "shades of meaning" to use the language of the Standards. Use words applicable to your grade level and write them on sentence strips, index cards or sticky notes. Give each student a word and they line up in their perceived order of where the word belongs. For example, words showing the outside temperature might include (in this order from the hottest to the coldest) boiling, hot, warm, lukewarm, cool, cold, freezing. Verbs (as stated in the Standard above) might include stroll, walk, jog, run.

What is your favorite vocabulary teaching tool that you currently use? Does it fit in with any of these standards?

Some of My Favorite Children's Books for Standards L.K.5a, L.K.5d, L.1.5a, L.1.5d, L.2.5a, and L.2.5b
Voices in the Park   By Anthony Brown   *Max's Words*   By Kate Banks, Illustrated by Boris Kulikov   *The Boy Who Loved Words*   By Roni Schotter, Illustratd by Giselle Potter   *Donovan's Word Jar*   By Monalisa Degross, Illustrated by Cheryl Hanna   *I Love My Hair!*   By Natasha Anastasia Tarpley, Illustrated by E. B. Lewis   *Miss Alaineus: A Vocabulary Disaster*   Written and Illustrated by Debra Frasier   *How Do Dinosaurs Eat Their Food?*   By Jane Yolen, Illustrated by Mark Teague

Think About It

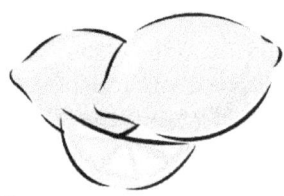

Inspiration

I have been fortunate to hear Maya Angelou speak two different times and have used many of her quotations in my work with teachers. I think you will appreciate one of my favorites. Ask me about the lemon that was given to me…

What Do I Want to Keep As Is?

What Do I Need to Add, Get Rid of, or Revise?

NOTES:

- Do I want my grade level to work together to set up a pacing guide or for weekly planning?
- How will I support my struggling students?
- How will I support my advanced learners?

© Gudwin, D. www.denise.gudwin.org

And…

THREE THOUGHTS

Between kindergarten and twelfth grade, high achievers have an average of 3.2 influential teachers, while low achievers have only 1.5 such teachers.

Nevertheless, research reveals that high achievers and low achievers perceive the characteristics of influential teachers in almost identical ways.

Ruddell (1999) Teaching Children to Read and Write: Becoming an Influential Teacher

---

Our job is to teach the kids we have…
- Not the ones we would like to have…
- Not the ones we used to have…
- Those we have right now.
- ALL of them

Source Unknown

Let's not just list
what we want our students to do,
but instead,
share with them
what we want them to learn, and why
- as we teach the Common Core
Standards to our children.

REFLECT...

Do you have some new children's books to share with your students in a purposefully planned Common Core Standard lesson?

Do you have at least one new Common Core strategy to try in the next few days?

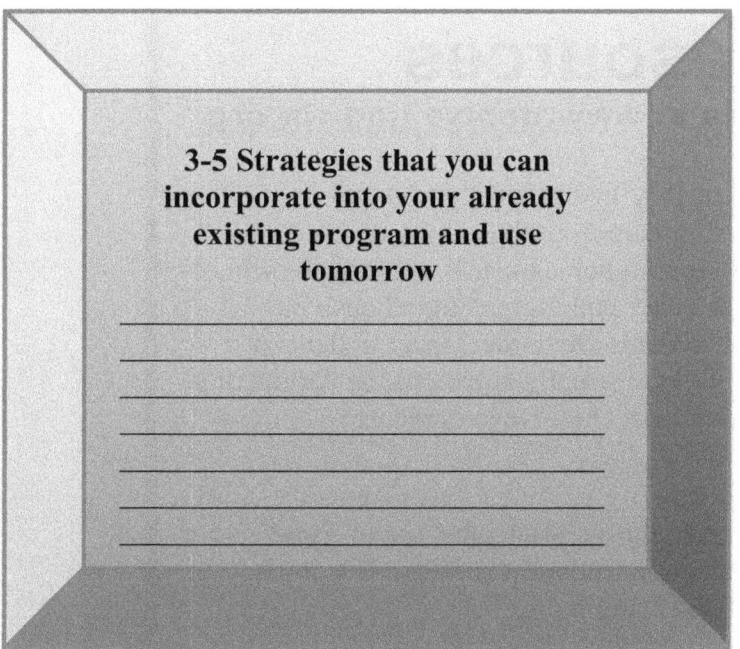

3-5 Strategies that you can incorporate into your already existing program and use tomorrow

WHY ARE WE HERE/ EXPECTATIONS MET?

Oral discussion about teachers' perception and teaching experiences often lead to a sense of professional excitement and renewed joy and energy related to their work.
Costa and Garmston, 1994

AND, ABOVE ALL... REMEMBER...
The main factor
that *really* affects student achievement
is the **effectiveness of the teacher.**

© Gudwin, D. www.denise.gudwin.org

Feel free to contact me for assistance at your school site; I am available to conduct this same seminar or one tailored to your school's needs:
denisegudwinconsulting@gmail.com
or through www.denise.gudwin.org (see website for CV and descriptions of seminars often requested.)

Excellent Online Resources

Check for updates at www.denise.gudwin.org

www.ascd.org/public-policy/common-core.aspx
 ASCD is an endorsing partner of the common core initiative. "The newer, higher standards will require schools and communities to better and more comprehensively support learning if students are to meet these enhanced expectations." (ASCD is formally known as the Association for Supervision and Curriculum Development)

benchmarkeducation.com
 Genre Studies, Metacognitive Strategies, use of Think Alouds with prompts to introduce a strategy, Benchmark Literacy, leveled books, and more

www.bestevidence.org
 "Empowering educators with evidence on proven programs" BEE Researchers the Recipient of the American Education Research Association (AERA) Award.

www.ciera.org
 Center for the Improvement of Early Reading Achievement (CIERA)

www.commoncore.org/maps/unit/grade_k_unit_2
 Common Core Curriculum Maps and lesson plans

http://commoncore.org/maps/unit/grade_2_unit_3
 Common Core Curriculum Maps and lesson plans

http://www.corestandards.org/the-standards/english-language-arts-standards/introduction/key-design-considerations/
> English Language Arts Standards – Introduction – Key Design Considerations. Part of the Introduction, including some of the background information

http://www.corestandards.org/assets/Appendix_A.pdf
> Research supporting key elements of the Standards. Includes extensive information on Text Complexity, as well as supplements for Reading Foundational Skills, and information for each of the strands.

http://www.corestandards.org/assets/Appendix_B.pdf
> Includes exemplars of reading text complexity, quality, and range and sample performance tasks related to Core Standards

http://commoncore.org/maps/documents/Pacing_Guide_K_1-3.pdf
> Provides the pacing chart for Reading Foundations for K, and levels 1-3.

www.denise.gudwin.org
> My website, with pictures of the professional books mentioned and the children's book used in this seminar. Also my CV (Curriculum Vita) and descriptions of seminars I can conduct at your school or district. My website is updated throughout the year, so check back from time to time. (As requested by previous seminar participants, I have linked the books right to Amazon, so you can find them on my website and click on them to order if you would like. And yes, I have the chimes available for you too, as many have requested!) I would like to add a page of successful teaching and learning environments, so if you find a strategy particularly successful and want to share, please email me details and pictures and I will get them up on my website. It will be a showcase for you and your school. Lets share our wonderful ideas and success stories!

www.fcrr.org
> Florida Center for Reading Research includes a wealth of information, including interventions and assessments, reports and research

www.getreadytoread.org
    Initiative of the National Center for Learning Disabilities' information for building the early literacy skills of preschool children.

www.interventioncentral.org.
    Intervention Central. Resource for Chart Dog and OKAPI! The Internet Application for Creating Curriculum-Based Assessment Reading Probe and much more

Itunes.apple.com/us/app/storykit/id329374595?mt=8
    Story Kit, a free application available from iTunes
    W.K.1., W.K.2, and/or **W.K.3**

www.kaganonline.com.
    Student engagement and learning.

www.k8accesscenter.org.
    The Access Center, U.S. Department of Education's Office of Special Education Programs. Research-based strategies

www.lesn.appstate.edu/fryeem/RE4030.friendly_letter_minilesson.htm
    Friendly Letter Mini-Lesson
    L.2.2b

www.livebinders.com/play/play/84777
    School Librarians and the Common Core Standards: Resources. Librarian resources are a bonus to reading teachers!

www.naeyc.org
    National Association for the Education of Young Children (NAEYC)

www.nationalreadingpanel.org.
    National Reading Panel

www.ncld.org
    National Center for Learning Disabilities

www.netlibrary.com.
    Full-text and professional books

NOTES:

www.nifl.gov
    National Institute for Literacy (NIFL). Literacy support

www.readwritethink.org
    Read Write Think – International Reading Association (IRA) and National Council of Teachers of English (NCTE). Offers classroom resources and professional development information. (Poetry Portfolios: Using Poetry to Teach Reading **RL.K.5** www.readwritethink.org/classroom-resources/lesson-plans/poetry-portfolios-using-poetry-152.html) and Letter Generator **W.2.6, L.2.2b** http://www.readwritethink.org/parent-afterschool-resources/games-tools/letter-generator-a-30187.html

www.reading.org.
    International Reading Association, International Organization

www.readingrockets.org
    Reading Rockets, National multimedia project for teachers of struggling readers (**RL.K.6** Reading Rockets www.readingrockets.org/books/interviews/depaola)

http://reading.uoregon.edu/curricula/or_rfc_review_2.php.
    Reading programs and research for whole class and small groups

www.swis.org.
    School-Wide Information System

www.texasreading.org
    University of Texas, Center for Reading and Language Arts. Wealth of information

www.tickettoread.com
    Voyager site for reading, vocabulary, questions, fluency. Motivational for students

www.w-w-c.org.
    What Works Clearinghouse, U.S. Department of Education's Institute of Education Sciences. Research reviews, interventions, and curriculum.

Many of the Children's Books and Professional Books used in activities and shown at the seminar are available at www.denise.gudwin.org

Children's Books
Referenced to Standards in the Handbook or During the Seminar

- *A Chair for My Mother* by Vera B. Williams and Caroline Binch
- *Abuela* by Authur Dorros
- *Alexander and the Terrible, Horrible, No Good, Very Bad Day* by Judith Viorst
- *All the Colors of the Earth* by Sheila Hamanaka
- *Amazing Grace* by Mary Hoffman and Caroline Binch
- *Anansi and the Moss Covered Rock* by Eric Kimmel
- *Angelina Ballerina* by Katherine Holabird
- *Animals Should Definitely Not Wear Clothing* by Judi Barrett
- *Anno's Counting Book* by Mitsumasa Anno
- *Are You My Mother?* By P.D. Eastman
- *Arlene Alda's 1-2-3: What Do You See?* By Arlene Alda
- *Ask Mr. Bear* by Marjorie Flack
- *Beatrice's Goat* by Page McBrier and Lori Lohstoeter
- *Bread and Jam for Frances* by Russell Hoban
- *Bridges* (See More Readers) by Seymour Simon
- *Bridges Are To Cross* by Philemon Sturges and Giles Laroche
- *Bridges: Amazing Structures to Design, Build & Test* by Carol A. Johmann, Elizabeth Rieth, and Michael P. Kline
- *Brown Bear, Brown Bear* by Bill Martin
- *Buzz* by Janet Wong
- *Can You Count Ten Toes? Count to Ten in Ten Different Languages* by Lezlie Evans and Denis Roche
- *Caps for Sale* by Esphyr Slobodkina
- *Carl Goes to Daycare* by Alexandra Day

NOTES:

- *Cars and Trucks and Things that Go* by Richard Scarry
- *Chalk* by Bill Thomson
- *Chameleon, Chamelion* by Joy Cowley and Nic Bishop
- *Charlotte's Web* by E.B. White and Garth Williams
- *Chicka Chicka 1, 2, 3* by Bill Martin, Jr., Michael Sampson, and Lois Ehlert
- *Chicka, Chicka, Boom, Boom* by Bill Martin
- *Corduroy* by Don Freeman
- *Curious George* by H. A. Rey
- *Dear Max* by Sally Grindley andTony Ross
- *Dear Mrs. LaRue* by Mark Teague
- *Dim Sum for Everyone!* By Grace Lin
- *Donovan's Word Jar* by Monalisa Degross and Cheryl Hanna
- *Farm Animals (Young Nature Series)* by Felicity Everett
- *Farmer Duck* by Martin Waddell
- *Feathers for Lunch* by Lois Ehlert
- *Four Feet, Two Sandals* by Karen Lynn Williams, Khadra Mohammed, and Doug Chayka
- *Freight Train* by Donald Crews
- *Frog and Toad Are Friends* by Arnold Lobel
- *Frog Goes to Dinner* by Mercer Mayer
- *George and Martha: The Complete Stories of Two Best Friends* by James Marshall
- *Go Away, Big Green Monster!* By Ed Emberley
- *Goats (Animals That Live on the Farm)* by JoAnn Early Macken
- *Goin' Someplace Special* by Pat McKissack
- *Goldilocks and the Three Bears* by Jan Brett
- *Good Dog, Carl* by Alexandra Day
- *Good Night, Gorilla* by Peggy Rathmann
- *Goodnight Moon* by Margaret Wise Brown
- *Grandfather Counts* by Andrea Cheng
- *Grandfather's Journey* by Allen Say
- *Guess How Much I Love You* by Sam McBratney
- *Happy Birthday, Moon* by Frank Asch
- *Harold and the Purple Crayon* by Crockett Johnson
- *Harry, the Dirty Dog* by Gene Zion
- *Henry and Mudge: The First Book* by Cynthia Rylant and Sucie Stevenson
- *Hi, Pizza Man!* by Virginia Walter
- *Horrible Harry Bugs the Three Bears* by Suzy Kline and Frank Remkiewicz
- *How Do Dinosaurs Eat Their Food?* by Jane Yolen and Mark Teague

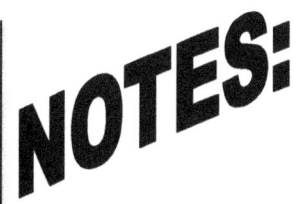

- *How Do I Put It On?* by Shigeo Watanabe
- Hush! A Thai Lullaby by Minfong Ho
- *I Am the Dog I am the Cat* by Donald Hall and Barry Moser
- *I Love My Hair!* by Natasha Anastasia Tarpley and E. B. Lewis
- *I Love You Like Crazy Cakes* by Rose Lewis
- *I Took My Frogs to the Library* by Eric Kimmel
- *I Wanna Iguana* by Karen Kaufman Orloff and David Catrow
- If Not for the Cat by Jack Prelutsky and Ted Rand
- *If You Give a Mouse a Cookie* by Laura Numeroff
- *Imogene's Antlers* by David Small
- *Is it Red? Is it Yellow? Is it Blue? An Adventure in Color* by Tana Hoban
- *Is Your Mama a Llama?* By Deborah Guarina
- *It Looked Like Spilt Milk* by Charles Shaw
- *Jump, Frog, Jump!* By Robert Kalan
- *Kites Sail High: A Book About Verbs* by Ruth Heller
- *Lilly's Purple Plastic Purse* by Kevin Henkes
- *Listen to the Rain* by Bill Martin Jr., John Archambault, and James Endicott
- *Little Blue and Little Yellow* by Leo Lionni
- *Lizard's Song* by George Shannon
- *Llama Llama Red Pajama* by Anna Dewdney
- *Looking Closely Along the Shore* by Frank Serafini
- *Lunch* by Denise Fleming
- *Lyle, Lyle Crocodile* by Bernard Waber
- *Mackinac Bridge: The Story of the Five-Mile Poem* by Gloria Whelan and Gijsbert van Frankenhuyzen
- *Madeline* by Ludwig Bemelmans
- *Make Way for Ducklings* by Robert McCloskey
- *Mama Zooms* by Jane Cowen-Fletcher
- *Martha Speaks* by Susan Meddaugh
- *Martin's Big Words: The Life of Martin Luther King, Jr.* by Doreen Rappaport
- *Max's Words* by Kate Banks and Boris Kulikov
- *Mike Mulligan and His Steam Shovel* by Virginia Lee Burton
- *Millions of Cats* by Wanda Gag
- *Miss Alaineus: A Vocabulary Disaster* by Debra Frasier
- *Moja Means One: Swahili Counting Book* by Muriel and Tom Feelings
- *More Parts* by Ted Arnold
- *Mouse Paint* by Ellen Stoll Walsh

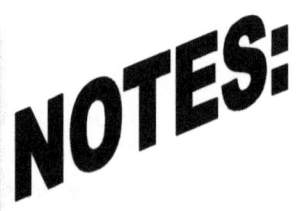

- *Mousetrap* by Diane Snowball and Kathi Ember
- *Mr. Grumpy's Outing* by John Burningham
- *My Big Dog* by Janet Stevens and Susan Stevens Crummel
- *My Father's Shop* by Satomi Ichikawa
- *My Rotten Red Headed Older Brother* by Patricia Polacco
- *Noisy Nora* by Rosemary Wells
- *Non Fiction Nature Treasure: A First Look at the Natural World* by Lizann Flatt
- *On Market Street* by Anita Lobel
- *On The Day I Was Born* by Debbi Chocolate
- *One Green Apple* by Eve Bunting and Ted Lewin
- *One Is a Drummer: A Book of Numbers* by Roseanne Thong and Grace Lin
- *One Is a Snail, Ten Is a Crab: A Counting by Feet Book* by April Pulley Sayre, Jeff Sayre, and Randy Cecil
- *Our Animal Friends at Maple Hill Farm* by Alice and Martin Provensen
- *Out of the Ocean* by Debra Frasier
- *Over in the Meadow* by John Langstaff
- *Owen and Mzee: The Language of Friendship* by Isabella and Craig Hatkoff, Paula Kahumbu, and Peter Greste
- *Owen and Mzee: The True Story of a Remarkable Friendship* by Isabella and Craig Hatkoff, Paula Kahumbu, and Peter Greste
- *Owl Moon* by Jane Yolen
- *Pancakes for Breakfast* by Tomie DePaola
- *Picasso and Minou* by P. I. Maltbie and Pau Estrada
- *Pigs (Animals That Live on the Farm)* by JoAnn Early Macken
- *Pigs Aplenty, Pigs Galore* by David McPhail
- *Pigs* by Gail Gibbons
- *Pop's Bridge* by Eve Bunting and C.F. Payne
- *Raven* by Gerald McDermott
- *Rosie's Walk* by Pat Hutchins
- *Seven Blind Mice* by Ed Young
- *Shades of Black* by Sandra Pinkney
- *Silent Music* by James Rumford
- *Snapshots from the Wedding* by Gary Soto
- *Snow in Jerusalem* by Deborah da Costa, Ying-Hwa Hu, and Cornelius Van Wright
- *Stone Soup* by Marcia Brown
- *Sylvester and the Magic Pebble* by William Steig

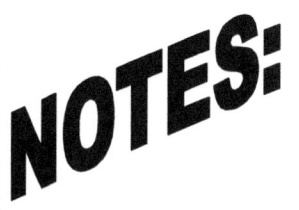

- *Tacky the Penguin* by Helen Lester
- *Tarra and Bella: The Elephant and Dog Who Became Best Friends* by Carol Buckley
- *Ten Apples Up on Top!* By Dr. Seuss
- *Ten Black Dots* by Donald Crews
- *Ten, Nine, Eight* by Molly Bang
- *The Ant and the Elephant* by Bill Peet
- *The Boy Who Loved Words* by Roni Schotter and Giselle Potter
- *The Bridge Builder* by Will Allen Dromgoole
- *The Carrot Seed* by Ruth Krauss
- *The Cat in the Hat* by Dr. Seuss
- *The Caterpillar and the Polliwog* by Jack Kent
- *The Complete Poems* by Christina Rossetti (Poem: Mix a Pancake)
- *The Cricket in Times Square* by George Selden and Garth Williams
- *The Day Jimmy's Boa Ate the Wash* by Trinka Noble
- *The Day of Ahmed's Secret by* Florence P. Heide, Judith H. Gilliland and Ted Lewin
- *The Empty Pot* by Demi
- *The Fire Cat* by Esther Holden Averill
- *The Girl Who Loved Wild Horses* by Paul Goble
- *The Lady with the Alligator Purse* by Nadine Westcott
- *The Library* by Sarah Stewart and David Small
- *The Little Engine that Could* by Watty Piper
- *The Little Mouse, the Red Ripe Strawberry, and the Big Hungry Bear by* Audrey Woods and Don Woods
- *The Little Painter of Sabana Grande* by Patricia Maloney Markun and Robert Casilla
- *The Mitten* by Jan Brett
- *The Napping House* by Audrey Wood
- *The Night Tree* by Eve Bunting and Ted Rand
- *The Oxford Illustrated Book of American Children's Poems* by Eliza Lee Follen (Poem: Three Little Kittens
- *The Recess Queen* by Alexis O'Neil and Laura Huliska-Beith
- *The Red Book* by Barbara Lehman
- *The Relatives Came* by Cynthia Rylant
- *The Seashore Book b*y Charlotte Zolotow and Wendell Minor
- *The Snowy Day* by Ezra Jack Keats
- *The Story of Babar, the Little Elephant* by Jean de Brunhoff
- *The Talk of Peter Rabbit* by Beatrix Potter
- *The Teddy Bears' Picnic* by Jimmy Kennedy

- *The Three Billy Goats Gruff* by Paul Galdone
- *The Three Cabritos* by Eric A. Kimmel and Stephen Gilpin
- *The Three Little Javelinas: Los Tres Pequenos Jabalies* (bilingual) by Susan Lowell
- *The Three Little Pigs* by James Marshall
- *The Three Little Wolves and the Big Bad Pig* by Eugene Trivizas and Helen Oxenbury
- *The Three Pigs* by David Wiesner
- *The True Story of the Three Little Pigs* by Jon Scieszka and Lane Smith
- *The Very Hungry Caterpillar* by Eric Carle
- *The Wolf's Chicken Stew* by Keiko Kasza
- *The Year at Maple Hill Farm* by Alice and Martin Provensen
- *There Was an Old Lady Who Swallowed a Fly* by Simms Taback
- *Three Cool Kids* by Rebecca Emberley
- *Throw Your Tooth on the Roof: Tooth Traditions From Around the World* by Selby Beeler
- *Tomorrow's Alphabet* by George Shannon and Donald Crews
- *Voices in the Park* by Anthony Brown
- *We're Going on a Bear Hunt* by Michael Rosen
- *What Color is Nature?* by Stepen R. Swinburne
- *When I Was Young in the Mountains* by Cynthia Rylant and Diane Goode
- *Where the Wild Things Are* by Maurice Sendak
- *Where's Spot* by Eric Hill
- *Who's Counting?* By Nancy Tafuri
- *Whose Hat?* By Margaret Miller
- *Whose Mouse are You?* By Robert Kraus
- *You Read to Me, I'll Read to You* by John Ciardi and Edward Gorey
- *You Read to Me, I'll Read to you: Very Short Fables to Read Together* by Mary Ann Hoberman and Michael Emberley
- *You Read to Me, I'll Read to you: Very Short Fairy Tales to Read Together* by Mary Ann Hoberman and Michael Emberley
- *You Read to Me, I'll Read to You: Very Short Stories to Read Together* by Mary Ann Hoberman and Michael Emberley
- *Zen Shorts* by Jon J. Muth
- *Zin! Zin! Zin! A Violin* by Lloyd Moss and Marjorie Priceman

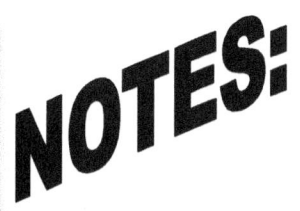

References

Check for updates at www.denise.gudwin.org SEE many of the book covers of the following references on my website. Children's Books shared today (and more) can also be found at my website.

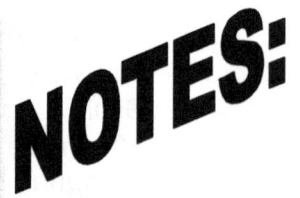

Adams, M.J., Foorman, B., Lundberg, I., and Beeler, T. (1998). *Phonemic awareness in young children.* Baltimore, MD: Paul H. Brookes Publishing Co.

Ainsworth, L. (2003). *Unwrapping the standards: A simple process to make standards manageable.* Englewood, CO: Lead + Learn Press

Allen, J. (2004). *Tools for teaching content literacy.* Portland, ME: Stenhouse.

Allen, J. (2002). *On the same page: Shared reading beyond the primary grades.* Portland, ME: Stenhouse Publishers.

Allen, J. (2000). *Yellow brick roads: Shared and guided paths to independent reading 4-12.* Portland, ME: Stenhouse Publishers.

Allen, J. (1999). *Words, words, words: Teaching vocabulary in grades 4-12.* Portland, ME: Stenhouse.

Allington, R. (2001). *What really matters for struggling readers: Designing research-based programs.* NY: Longman.

Allington, R. and Cunningham, P. (1996). *Schools that work: Where all children read and write.* Upper Saddle River, NJ: Pearson Education.

Athans, S. K., & Devine, D. A., (2010). *Fun-tastic activities for differentiating comprehension instruction grades 2-6.* Newark, DE: International Reading Association.

Beck, I., McKeown, M., and Kucan, L. (2002). *Bringing words to life: Robust vocabulary instruction.* NY: Guilford Press.

Bender, W. & Larkin, M. (2009). *Reading strategies for elementary students with learning difficulties: Strategies for RTI.* Thousand Oaks, CA: Corwin Press.

Boushey, G., & Moser, J. (2006). *The Daily Five.* Portland, ME: Stenhouse Publishers.

Brown, H. and Cambourne, B. (1990). *Read and retell.* Portsmouth, NH: Heinemann.

Burkins, J M. & Croft, M. M., (2010). *Preventing misguided reading: New strategies for guided reading teachers.* Newark, DE: International Reading Association and Thousand Oaks, CA: Corwin Press.

Burns, S., Griffin, P., and Snow, C. (1999). (Ed.). *Starting out right: A guide to promoting children's reading success.* Washington, DC: National Academy Press.

Center for the Improvement of Early Reading Achievement (CIERA). (1998).

Cheyney, W., Cohen, E. J., & Gudwin, D. (2007). *Phonological awareness and early literacy assessment, PreK.* Chicago, IL: Wright Group/McGraw-Hill.

Cooper, (2000). *Literacy: Helping children construct meaning.* Boston, MA: Houghton Mifflin Company.

Costa, A. and Garmston, R. (1994). *Cognitive coaching: A foundation for renaissance schools.* Norwood, MA: Christopher-Gordon Publishers.

Cramer, E., Gudwin, D., and Salazar, M. (2007). Professional development: Assisting urban schools in making Annual Yearly Progress. *Journal of Urban Learning, Teaching, and Research. AERA* 3, 13-24.

Crawford, J. (2011). *Using power standards to build an aligned curriculum: A process manual.* Thousand Oaks, CA: Corwin

Cunningham, P. (2009). *Phonics they use: Words for reading and writing.* Boston: Pearson.

Cunningham, P. (2000) *Systematic sequential phonics they use: For beginning readers of all ages.* Greensboro, NC: Carson-Dellosa Publishing Company.

Cunningham, P., and Allington, R. (2010). *Classrooms that work: They can all read and write.* (5th Ed.). NY: Longman.

Cunningham, P. and Hall, D. (1997) *Month by month phonics for first grade: Systematic, multilevel instruction.* Greensboro, NC: Carson-Dellosa Publishing Company.

Dorn, L. J., French, C., & Jones, T., (1998). *Apprenticeship in literacy: Transitions across reading and writing.* Portland, ME: Stenhouse Publishers.

Dorn, L. J., & Soffos, C., (2005). *Teaching for deep comprehension: A reading workshop approach.* Portland, ME: Stenhouse Publishers.

Drake, S. (2007). *Standards-based integrated curriculum: Aligning curriculum, content, assessment, and instruction.* Thousand Oaks, CA: Corwin Press.

Duffy-Hester, A. (1999). Teaching struggling readers in elementary school classrooms: A review of classroom reading programs and principles for instruction. *The Reading Teacher, 52* (5), 480-495.

Duke, N. (2003). Reading to learn from the very beginning: Information books in early childhood. *National Association for the Education of Young Children. Journal.naeyc.org/btj/200303/InformationBooks.pdf.best best*

Farr, R., & Conner, J., *Using think-alouds to improve reading comprehension.* Retrieved from www.readingrockets.org/article/102

Fisher, D. & Frey, N (2008). *Better learning through structured teaching: A framework for the gradual release of responsibility.* Alexandria, VA: Association for Supervision and Curriculum Development.

Fogarty, R. (2009). *Brain-compatible classrooms.* Thousand Oaks, CA: Corwin Press.

Fox, M. (2001). *Reading magic: Why reading aloud to our children will change their lives forever.* San Diego, CA: Harvest/Harcourt.

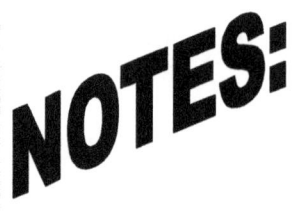

NOTES:

Friend, M., & Bursuck, W. (2006). *Including students with special needs: A practical guide for classroom teachers.* Boston, MA: Allyn and Bacon.

Graves, M. (2009). *Teaching individual words: One size does not fit all.* (Joint publication) New York: Teachers College Press and Newark: DE: The International Reading Association.

Gudwin, D. M. (2002). *A qualitative study of the perceptions of six preservice teachers: Implementing oral and written retelling strategies in teaching reading to students with learning disabilities.* Paper Presented at Eastern Educational Research Association Conference, Teacher Education Division, Sarasota, Florida. Eric Document # ED 466896.

Gudwin, D. M. (2008). *Accelerating the reading achievement of students with learning disabilities: Strategies that work.* WA: Bureau of Education and Research.

Gudwin D., & Salazar, M. (2010). *Mentoring & coaching: A lifeline for teachers in a multicultural setting.* Thousand Oaks, CA: Corwin Press.

Gunning, T. G. (2002). *Creating literacy instruction for all children.* Needham Heights, MA: Allyn and Bacon.

Hale, J. & Dunlap, Jr. R. (2010). *An educational leader's guide to curriculum mapping: Creating and sustaining collaborative cultures.* Thousand Oaks, CA: Corwin .

Hall, S., and Moats, L.C. (Spring 2000). Why reading to children is important. *American Educator.*

Hart, B and Risley, T. (1995). *Meaningful differences in the everyday experience of young American children.* Baltimore, MD: Paul H. Brookes.

Hebert, C. R. (2008). *Catch a falling reader.* Thousand Oaks, CA: Corwin Press.

Hill, B. C., Johnson, N. & Schlick Noe, K., (1995). *Literature circles and response.* Norwood, MA: Christopher-Gordon Publishers.

Hill, B. C., Schlick Noe, K., & Johnson, N. (2000). *Literature*

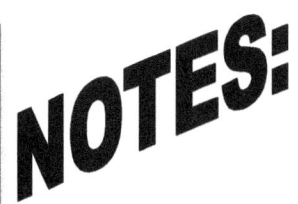

circles resource guide. Norwood, MA: Christopher-Gordon Publishers.

Honig, B., Diamond, L., & Gutlohn, L. (2000). *Teaching reading sourcebook: For kindergarten through eighth grade.* Novato, CA: Arena Press and Emeryville, CA: CORE.

Hoyt, L. (1999). *Revisit, reflect, retell: Strategies for improving reading comprehension.* Portsmouth, NH: Heinemann.

Jackson, R. R. (2009). *Never work harder than your students & other principles of great teaching.* Alexandria, VA: Association for Supervision and Curriculum Development.

Jobe & Dayton-Sakari (1999). *Reluctant readers: Connecting students and books for successful reading experiences.* Ontario: Pembroke Publishers.

Kendall, J. (2011). *Understanding common core state standards.* Alexandria, VA: Association for Supervision and Curriculum Development and Denver, CO: McREL

Keene, E. & Zimmerman, S. (1997). *Mosaic of thought.* Portsmouth, NH: Heinemann.

Lanning, L. A. (2009). *4 powerful strategies for struggling readers grades 3-8: Small-group instruction that improves comprehension.* Thousand Oaks, CA: Corwin Press.

Lauren, J. (1997). *Succeeding with LD (learning differences): 20 true stories about real people with LD.* Minneapolis, MN: Free Spirit Publishing.

Lyon, G.R. (1998). Why reading is not a natural process. *Educational Leadership 55* (6), 14-18.

McKenna, M. C. & Stahl, S. A. (2003). *Assessment for reading instruction.* New York: Guilford Press.

Makas, E. (2009). *From mandate to achievement: 5 steps to a curriculum system that works!* Thousand Oaks, CA: Corwin

Manzo, A. and Manzo, U., (1993). *Literacy disorders: Holistic diagnosis and remediation.* Fort Worth, TX: Harcourt Brace Jovanovich College Publishers.

NOTES:

Marzano, R. J., (2007). *The art and science of teaching: A comprehensive framework for effective instruction.* Alexandria, VA: Association for Supervision and Curriculum Development.

Miami Dade County Public Schools. Division of Language Arts/Reading. *The comprehensive reading plan/best practices in elementary reading manual.* Available at 1500 Biscayne Boulevard. Miami, FL 33132.

Moats, L. (1999). *Teaching reading is rocket science: What expert teachers of reading should know and be able to do.* Washington, DC: America Federation of Teachers.

Morrow, L. (1997). *Literacy development in the early years: Helping children read and write.* (3rd Ed.). Boston, MA: Allyn and Bacon.

Moss, B. & Young, T. A., (2010). *Creating lifelong readers through independent reading.* Newark, DE: International Reading Association.

Palinscar, A., and Brown, A. (1984). Reciprocal teaching of comprehension-fostering and comprehension-monitoring activities. *Cognition and Instruction, 1, 2.*

Pearson, P.D. & Gallagher, M.C. (1983). The instruction of reading comprehension. *Contemporary Education Psychology 8:* 317-344.

Pressley, M. (2002). *Reading instruction that works.* NY: Guilford Publications, Inc.

Pressley, M., Wharton-McDonald, R., Allington, R., Morrow, L.M., & Block, C.C. (2001). *Learning to read: Lessons from exemplary first grade classrooms.* NY: Guilford Publications.

Psencik, K. (2009). *Accelerating student and staff learning: Purposeful curriculum collaboration.* Thousand Oaks, CA: Corwin.

Rasinski, T. (2003). *The fluent reader: Oral reading strategies for building word recognition, fluency, and comprehension.* NYC, NY: Scholastic.

Reeves, D. (2009). *Leading change in your school: How to conquer myths, build commitment, and get results.* Alexandria, VA: ASCD.

Reeves, D. (2011). *Getting reading for common standards.* American School Board Jounral. Retrieved from wwwleadandlearn.com/sites/default/files/articles/1103-asbj-getting-ready-common-standards.pdf.

Routman, R. (2003). *Reading essentials.* Portsmouth, NH: Heinemann.

Ruddell, R. (1999). *Teaching children to read and write: Becoming an influential teacher.* Needham Heights, MA: Allyn & Bacon.

Ruddell, R. and Ruddell (1995). *Teaching children to read and write: Becoming an influential teacher.* Needham Heights, MA: Allyn & Bacon.

Salazar, M., Gudwin, D., Nevin, A. (Spring, 2008) Special education mentor teacher leaders: Making a difference with beginning teachers *Florida Educational Leadership Journal (FASCD),* 50-56.

Santa, C., Havens, L., and Maycumber, E. (1996). *Project CRISS - Creating independence through student-owned strategies.* Dubuque, IA: Kendall/Hunt Publishing.

Schlick Noe, K. & Johnson, N. (1999). *Getting started with literature circles.* Norwood, MA: Christopher-Gordon Publishers.

Serafini, F. (2004). *Lessons in comprehension: Explicit instruction in the reading workshop.* Portsmouth, NH: Heinemann.

Serafini, F. (2010). *Classroom reading assessment: More efficient ways to view and evaluate your students.* Portsmouth, NH: Heinemann.

Soto-Hinman, I., & Hetzel, J. (2009). *The literacy gaps: Bridge-building strategies for English language learners and standard English learners.* Thousand Oaks, CA: Corwin Press.

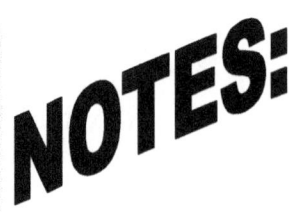

Stronge, J. (2010). *Qualities of effective teachers.* Alexandria, VA: Association for Supervision and Curriculum Development.

Stuhlman, M.W. & Pianta, R.C. (2009). Profiles of educational quality in first grade. *Elementary School Journal, 109*(4), 323-342.

Tierney and Readence (2000). *Content area literacy: An integrated approach.* Dubuque, IA: Kendall/Hunt.

Tomlinson, C.A. (2000). Reconcilable differences? Standards-based teaching and differentiation. *Educational Leadership, 58* (1). 6-11.

Torgesen, J. K. (Spring/Summer 1998). Catch them before they fall: Identification and assessment to prevent reading failure in young children. *American Educator, 22,* 32-39.

Tovani, C. (2000). *I read it, but I don't get it: Comprehension strategies for adolescent readers.* Portland, ME: Stenhouse.

Trelease, J. (2001). *The read aloud handbook.* New York: Penguin Books.

Voltz, D., Sims, M.J., & Nelson, B. (2010). *Connecting teachers students, and standards: Strategies for success in diverse and inclusive classrooms.* Alexandria, VA: Association for Supervision and Curriculum Development.

Walpole, S. & McKenna, M. C. (2004). *The literacy coach's handbook: A guide to research-based practice.* New York: Guilford Press.

Weber, S. (2008). *The benefits of unpacking the standards.* www.k12curriculumdevelopment.com/1/post/2009/8/unpacking-standards.html

Wong, H. and Wong, R. (1998). *How to be an effective teacher: The first days of school.* Mountain View, CA: Harry K. Wong Publications.

Zygouris-Coe, V., Wiggins, M, & Smith, L. (2004). Engaging students with text: The 3-2-1 strategy. *The Reading Teacher, 58*(4), 381-384.

Appendix

*Teacher Tools to Assist You
In Your Common Core Journey.*

"All autonomy is not lost: It is more important than ever for teachers to creatively engage students with effective instructional strategies and adapt content to the needs of the learners. If standards establish the 'what,' then teachers determine the 'how.'"
John Kendall, 2011

College and Career Readiness Anchor Standards for Reading	97
Reading Standards for Literature K-3 (RL)	99
Reading Standards for Informational Text K-3 (RI)	103
Reading Standards: Foundational Skills K-3 (FS)	107
Speaking and Listening Standards K-3 (Sample) (SL)	112
Language Standards K-3 (Sample) (L)	113
Common Core Standards Cited in Resource Handbook	114
Sample Mentor Texts with Author, Illustrator, Levels, and Description	115
Walk Through Another Standard	117
Self Reflection Questions	118
Independent Work Management Chart	119
Using Assessment Results: Monitoring and Grouping, Based on St Data	120
37 Rimes	121
Fluency Chunk	122
Fluency Norms	123
Quick Fluency Check	124
Learning Log Graphic Organizer	125
4-Point Story Board Graphic Organizer	126
6-Point Story Board Graphic Organizer	127
Two-Column Notes Graphic Organizer	128
Venn Diagram Graphic Organizer	129
Vocabulary Word Analysis Graphic Organizer	130
My Weekly Collection of Words, Words, Words	131
Character Analysis Graphic Organizer	132
Questions and Responding to Literature	133
Retelling Log Graphic Organizer	134
Think Alouds and Conversations	135
Accommodations Checklist	136
Reflective Note Pages	138
Ongoing TO-DO List	140

College and Career Readiness Anchor Standards for Reading

Source: Common Core State Standards Initiative www.corestandards.org/the-standards/english-language-arts-standards

READING STRANDS:

Key Ideas and Details Standards:
1. Read Closely to determine what the text says explicitly and to make logical inferences from the text
2. Determine central ideas or themes of a text and analyze their development; summarize the key supporting details and ideas.
3. Analyze how and why individuals, events, and ideas develop and interact over the course of a text.

Craft and Structure Standards:
4. Interpret words and phrases as they are used in a text, including determining technical, connotative, and figurative meanings, and analyze how specific word choices shape meaning or tone.
5. Analyze the structure of texts, including how specific sentences, paragraphs, and larger portions of the text (e.g. a section, chapter, scene, or stanza) relate to each other and the whole.
6. Assess how point of view or purpose shapes the content and style of a text.

Integration of Knowledge and Ideas Standards:
7. Integrate and evaluate content presented in diverse media and formats, including visually and quantitatively, as well as in words.
8. Delineate and evaluate the argument and specific claims in a text, including the validity of the reasoning as well as the relevance and sufficiency of the evidence.
9. Analyze how two or more texts address similar themes or topics in order to build knowledge or to compare the approaches the authors take.

Range of Reading and Level of Text Complexity Standard:
10. Read and comprehend complex literary and informational texts independently and proficiently

SPEAKING AND LISTENING STRANDS:

Comprehension and Collaboration Standards:
1. Prepare for and participate effectively in a range of conversations and collaborations with diverse partners, building on others' ideas and expressing their own clearly and persuasively.
2. Integrate and evaluate information presented in diverse media and formats, including visually, quantitatively, and orally.
3. Evaluate a speaker's point of view, reasoning, and use of evidence and rhetoric.

Presentation of Knowledge and Ideas Standards:

4. Present information, findings, supporting evidence such that listeners can follow the line of reasoning and the organization, development, and styles are appropriate to task, purpose, and audience.
5. Make strategic use of digital media and visual displays of data to express information and enhance understanding of presentations.
6. Adapt speech to a variety of contexts and communicative tasks, demonstrating command of formal English when indicated or appropriate.

LANGUAGE STRANDS:

Conventions of Standard English:
1. Demonstrate command of the conventions of standard English grammar and usage when writing or speaking.
2. Demonstrate command of the conventions of standard English capitalization, punctuation, and spelling when writing.

Knowledge of Language:
3. Apply knowledge of language to understand how language functions in different contexts, to make effective choices for meaning or style, and to comprehend more fully when reading or listening.

Vocabulary Acquisition and Use:
4. Determine or clarify the meaning of unknown and multiple-meaning words and phrases by using context clues, analyzing meaningful word parts, and consulting general and specialized reference materials.
5. Demonstrate understanding of figurative language, word relationships, and nuances in word meaning.
6. Acquire and use accurately a range of general academic and domain-specific words and phrases sufficient for reading, writing, speaking, and listening at the college and career readiness level; demonstrate independence in gathering vocabulary knowledge when encountering an unknown term important to comprehension or expression.

Reading Standards for Literature K-5 (RL) Source: Common Core State Standards Initiative
www.corestandards.org/the-standards/english-language-arts-standards

RL	Anchor Standards	Kindergarten Students	Grade 1 Students	Grade 2 Students	Grade 3 Students
Key Ideas & Details	1. Read Closely to determine what the text says explicitly & to make logical inferences from the text	RL.K.1 With prompting & support, ask & answer questions about key details in a text.	RL.1.1 Ask & answer questions about key details in a text.	RL.2.1 Ask & answer such questions as *who, what, where, when, why, & how* to demonstrate understanding of key details in a text.	RL.3.1 Ask & answer questions to demonstrate understanding of a text, referring explicitly to the text as the basis for the answers.
	2. Determine central ideas or themes of a text & analyze their development; summarize the key supporting details & ideas.	RL.K.2 With prompting & support, retell familiar stories, including key details.	RL.1.2 Retell stories, including key details, & demonstrate understanding of their central message or lesson.	RL.2.2 Recount stories, including fables & folktales from diverse cultures, & determine their central message, lesson, or moral.	RL.3.2 Recount stories, including fables, folktales, & myths from diverse cultures; determine the central message, lesson, or moral & explain how it is conveyed through key details in the text.
	3. Analyze how & why individuals, events, & ideas develop & interact over the course of a text.	RL.K.3 With prompting & support, identify characters, settings, & major events in a story.	RL.1.3 Describe characters, settings, & major events in a story, using key details.	RL.2.3 Describe how characters in a story respond to major events & challenges.	RL.3.3 Describe characters in a story (e.g., their traits, motivations, or feelings) & explain how their actions contribute to the sequence of events.

Reading Standards for Literature K-5 (RL – cont.)

RL	Anchor Standards	Kindergarten Students	Grade 1 Students	Grade 2 Students	Grade 3 Students
Craft & Structure	4. Interpret words & phrases as they are used in a text, including determining technical, connotative, & figurative meanings, & analyze how specific word choices shape meaning or tone.	RL.K.4 Ask & answer questions about unknown words in a text.	RL.1.4 Identify words & phrases in stories or poems that suggest feelings or appeal to the senses.	RL.2.4 Describe how words & phrases (e.g., regular beats, alliteration, rhymes, repeated lines) supply rhythm & meaning in a story, poem, or song.	RL.3.4 Determine the meaning of words & phrases as they are used in a text, distinguishing literal from nonliteral language.
	5. Analyze the structure of texts, including how specific sentences, paragraphs, & larger portions of the text (e.g., a section, chapter, scene, or stanza) relate to each other & the whole.	RL.K.5 Recognize common types of text (e.g., storybooks, poems).	RL.1.5 Explain major differences between books that tell stories & books that give information, drawing on a wide reading of a range of text types.	RL.2.5 Describe the overall structure of a story, including describing how the beginning introduces the story & the ending concludes the action.	RL.3.5 Refer to parts of stories, dramas, & poems when writing or speaking about a text, using terms such as chapter, scene, & stanza; describe how each successive part builds on earlier sections.
	6. Assess how point of view or purpose shapes the content & style of a text.	RL.K.6 With prompting & support, name the author & illustrator of a story & define the role of each in telling the story.	RL.1.6 Identify who is telling the story at various points in a text.	RL.2.6 Acknowledge differences in the points of view of characters, including by speaking in a different voice for each character when reading dialogue aloud.	RL.3.6 Distinguish their own point of view from that of the narrator or those of the characters.

Reading Standards for Literature K-5 (RL – cont.)

RL	Anchor Standards	Kindergarten Students	Grade 1 Students	Grade 2 Students	Grade 3 Students
Integration of Knowledge & Ideas * See "Research to Build and Present Knowledge" in Writing and "Comprehension and Collaboration" in Speaking and Listening for additional standards relevant to gathering, assessing, and applying information from print and digital sources.	7. Integrate & evaluate content presented in diverse media & formats, including visually & quantitatively, as well as in words.*	RL.K.7 With prompting & support, describe the relationship between illustrations & the story in which they appear (e.g., what moment in a story an illustration depicts).	RL.1.7 Use illustrations and details in a story to describe its characters, setting, or events.	RL.2.7 Use information gained from the illustrations and words in a print or digital text to demonstrate understanding of its characters, setting, or plot.	RL.3.7 Explain how specific aspects of a text's illustrations contribute to what is conveyed by the words in a story (e.g., create mood, emphasize aspects of a character or setting).
	8. Delineate & evaluate the argument & specific claims in a text, including the validity of the reasoning as well as the relevance & sufficiency of the evidence.	RL.K.8 (Not applicable to literature)	RL.1.8 (Not applicable to literature)	RL.2.8 (Not applicable to literature)	RL.3.8 (Not applicable to literature)
	9. Analyze how two or more texts address similar themes or topics in order to build knowledge or to compare the approaches the authors take.	RL.K.9 With prompting & support, compare and contrast the adventures and experiences of characters in familiar stories.	RL.1.9 Compare and contrast the adventures and experiences of characters in stories.	RL.2.9 Compare and contrast two or more versions of the same story (e.g., Cinderella stories) by different authors or from different cultures.	RL.3.9 Compare and contrast stories the themes, settings, and plots of stories written by the same author about the same or similar characters (e.g., in books from a series).

Reading Standards for Literature K-5 (RL – cont.)

RL	Anchor Standards	Kindergarten Students	Grade 1 Students	Grade 2 Students	Grade 3 Students
Range of Reading and Level of Text Complexity	**10. Read and comprehend complex literary and informational texts independently and proficiently.**	**RL.K.10** Actively engage in group reading activities with purpose and understanding.	**RL.1.10** With prompting and support, read prose and poetry of appropriate complexity for grade 1.	**RL.2.10** By the end of the year, read and comprehend literature, including stories and poetry, in the grades 2-3 text complexity band proficiently, with scaffolding as needed at the high end of the range.	**RL.3.10** By the end of the year, read and comprehend literature, including stories, dramas, and poetry, at the high end of the grades 2-3 text complexity band independently and proficiently.

Reading Standards for Informational Text K-5 (RI) Source: Common Core State Standards Initiative
www.corestandards.org/the-standards/english-language-arts-standards

RI	Anchor Standards	Kindergarten Students	Grade 1 Students	Grade 2 Students	Grade 3 Students
Key Ideas & Details	**1. Read Closely to determine what the text says explicitly & to make logical inferences from the text**	**RI.K.1** With prompting & support, ask & answer questions about key details in a text.	**RI.1.1** Ask & answer questions about key details in a text.	**RI.2.1** Ask & answer such questions as *who, what, where, when, why, & how* to demonstrate understanding of key details in a text.	**RI.3.1** Ask & answer questions to demonstrate understanding of a text, referring explicitly to the text as the basis for the answers.
	2. Determine central ideas or themes of a text & analyze their development; summarize the key supporting details & ideas.	**RI.K.2** With prompting & support, identify the main topic and retell key details of a text.	**RI.1.2** Identify the main topic and retell key details of a text.	**RI.2.2** Identify the main topic of a multiparagraph text as well as the focus of specific paragraphs within the text.	**RI.3.2** Determine the main idea of a text; recount the key details and explain how they support the main idea.
	3. Analyze how & why individuals, events, & ideas develop & interact over the course of a text.	**RI.K.3** With prompting & support, describe the connection between two individuals, events, ideas, or pieces of information in a text.	**RI.1.3** Describe the connection between two individuals, events, ideas, or pieces of information in a text.	**RI.2.3** Describe the connection between a series of historical events, scientific ideas or concepts, or steps in technical procedures in a text.	**RI.3.3** Describe the relationship between a series of historical events, scientific ideas or concepts, or steps in technical procedures in a text, using language that pertains to time, sequence, and cause/effect.

Reading Standards for Informational Text K-5 (RI – cont.)

RI	Anchor Standards	Kindergarten Students	Grade 1 Students	Grade 2 Students	Grade 3 Students
Craft & Structure	4. Interpret words & phrases as they are used in a text, including determining technical, connotative, & figurative meanings, & analyze how specific word choices shape meaning or tone.	RI.K.4 With prompting and support, ask and answer questions about unknown words in a text.	RI.1.4 Ask and answer questions to help determine or clarify the meaning of words and phrases in a text.	RI.2.4 Determine the meaning of words and phrases in a text relevant to a grade 2 topic or subject area.	RI.3.4 Determine the meaning of general academic and domain-specific words and phrases in a text relevant to a *grade 3 topic or subject area*.
	5. Analyze the structure of texts, including how specific sentences, paragraphs, & larger portions of the text (e.g., a section, chapter, scene, or stanza) relate to each other & the whole.	RI.K.5 Identify the front cover, back cover, and title page of a book.	RI.1.5 Know and use various text features (e.g., headings, tables of contents, glossaries, electronic menus, icons) to locate key facts or information in a text.	RI.2.5 Know and use various text features (e.g., captions, bold print, subheadings, glossaries, indexes, electronic menus, icons) to locate key facts or information in a text efficiently.	RI.3.5 Use text features and search tools (e.g., key words, sidebars, hyperlinks) to locate information relevant to a given topic efficiently.
	6. Assess how point of view or purpose shapes the content & style of a text.	RI.K.6 Name the author & illustrator of a text & define the role of each in presenting the ideas or information in a text.	RI.1.6 Distinguish between information provided by pictures or other illustrations and information provided by the words in a text.	RI.2.6 Identify the main purpose of a text, including what the author wants to answer, explain, or describe.	RI.3.6 Distinguish their own point of view from that of the author of a text.

Denise M. Gudwin, Ph.D. Appendix

Reading Standards for Informational Text K-5 (RI – cont.)

RI	Anchor Standards	Kindergarten Students	Grade 1 Students	Grade 2 Students	Grade 3 Students
Integration of Knowledge & Ideas

* See "Research to Build and Present Knowledge" in Writing and "Comprehension and Collaboration" in Speaking and Listening for additional standards relevant to gathering, assessing, and applying information from print and digital sources. | 7. Integrate & evaluate content presented in diverse media & formats, including visually & quantitatively, as well as in words.* | **RI.K.7** With prompting & support, describe the relationship between illustrations & the text in which they appear (e.g., what person, place, thing, or idea in the text an illustration depicts). | **RI.1.7** Use the illustrations and details in a text to describe its key ideas. | **RI.2.7** Explain how specific images (e.g., a diagram showing how a machine works) contribute to and clarify a text. | **RI.3.7** Use information gained from illustrations (e.g., maps, photographs) and the words in a text to demonstrate understanding of the text (e.g., where, when, why, and how key events occur). |
| | 8. Delineate & evaluate the argument & specific claims in a text, including the validity of the reasoning as well as the relevance & sufficiency of the evidence. | **RI.K.8** With prompting and support, identify the reasons an author gives to support points in a text. | **RI.1.8** Identify the reasons an author gives to support points in a text. | **RI.2.8** Describe how reasons support specific points the author makes in a text. | **RI.3.8** Describe the logical connection between particular sentences and paragraphs in a text (e.g., comparison, cause/effect, first/second/third in a sequence). |
| | 9. Analyze how two or more texts address similar themes or topics in order to build knowledge or to compare the approaches the authors take. | **RI.K.9** With prompting & support, identify basic similarities in and differences between two texts on the same topic (e.g., in illustrations, descriptions, or procedures). | **RI.1.9** Identify basic similarities in and differences between two texts on the same topic (e.g., in illustrations, descriptions, or procedures). | **RI.2.9** Compare and contrast the most important points presented by two texts on the same topic. | **RI.3.9** Compare and contrast the most important points and key details presented in two texts on the same topic. |

© Gudwin, D. www.denise.gudwin.org

Reading Standards for Informational Text K-5 (RI – cont.)

RI	Anchor Standards	Kindergarten Students	Grade 1 Students	Grade 2 Students	Grade 3 Students
Range of Reading and Level of Text Complexity	**10. Read and comprehend complex literary and informational texts independently and proficiently.**	**RI.K.10** Actively engage in group reading activities with purpose and understanding.	**RI.1.10** With prompting and support, read informational texts appropriately complex for grade 1.	**RI.2.10** By the end of the year, read and comprehend informational texts, including history/social studies, science, and technical texts, in the grades 2-3 text complexity band proficiently, with scaffolding as needed at the high end of the range.	**RI.3.10** By the end of the year, read and comprehend informational texts, including history/social studies, science, and technical texts, at the high end of the grades 2-3 text complexity band independently and proficiently.

Reading Standards: Foundational Skills
Source: Common Core State Standards Initiative
www.corestandards.org/the-standards/english-language-arts-standards

"These standards are directed toward fostering students' understanding and working knowledge of concepts of print, the alphabetic principle, and other basic conventions of the English writing system. These foundational skills are not an end in and of themselves; rather, they are necessary and important components of an effective, comprehensive reading program designed to develop proficient readers with the capacity to comprehend texts across a range of types and disciplines. Instruction should be differentiated: good readers will need much less practice with these concepts than struggling readers will. The point is to teach students what the need to learn and not what they already know – to discern when particular children or activities warrant more or less attention.

Note: In kindergarten, children are expected to demonstrate increasing awareness and competence in the areas that follow.

Reading Standards: Foundational Skills K-5 (FS)

FS	Kindergarten Students	Grade 1 Students
Print Concepts #1	**FS.K.1** Demonstrate understanding of the organization and basic feature of print. a. Follow words from left to right, top to bottom, and page by page. b. Recognize that spoken words are represented in written language by specific sequences of letters. c. Understand that words are separated by spaces in print. d. Recognize and name all upper- and lowercase letters of the alphabet.	**FS.1.1** Demonstrate understanding of the organization and basic features of print. a. Recognize the distinguishing features of a sentence (e.g., first word, capitalization, ending punctuation).

Reading Standards: Foundational Skills K-5 (FS – cont.)

FS	Kindergarten Students	Grade 1 Students
Phonological Awareness #2	**FS.K.2** Demonstrate understanding of spoken words, syllables, and sounds (phonemes). a. Recognize and produce rhyming words. b. Count, pronounce, blend, and segment syllables in spoken words. c. Blend and segment onsets and rimes of single-syllable spoken words. d. Isolate and pronounce the initial, medial vowel, and final sounds (phonemes) in three-phoneme (consonant-vowel-consonant, or CVC) words. * (This does not include CVC ending with /l/, /r/, or /x/.) e. Add or substitute individual sounds (phonemes) in simple, one-syllable words to make new words.	**FS.1.2** Demonstrate understanding of spoken words, syllables, and sounds (phonemes). a. Distinguish long from short vowel sounds in spoken single-syllable words. b. Orally produce single-syllable words by blending sounds (phonemes), including consonant blends. c. Isolate and pronounce initial, medial vowel, and final sounds (phonemes) in spoken single-syllable words. d. Segment spoken single-syllable words into their complete sequence of individual sounds (phonemes).

*Words, syllables, or phonemes written in /slashes/ refer to their pronunciation or phonology. Thus, /CVC/ is a word with three phonemes regardless of the number of letters in the spelling of the word.

Reading Standards: Foundational Skills K-5 (FS – cont.)

FS	Kindergarten Students	Grade 1 Students
Phonics and Word Recognition #3	**FS.K.3** Know and apply grade-level phonics and word analysis skills in decoding words. a. Demonstrate basic knowledge of one-to-one letter-sound correspondences by producing the primary or many of the most frequent sound for each consonant. b. Associate the long and short sounds with common spellings (graphemes) for the five major vowels. c. Read common high-frequency words by sight (e.g., *the, of, to, you, she, my, is, are, do, does*). d. Distinguish between similarly spelled words by identifying the sounds of the letters that differ.	**FS.1.3** Know and apply grade-level phonics and word analysis skills in decoding words. a. Know the spelling-sound correspondences for common consonant digraphs. b. Decode regularly spelled one-syllable words. c. Know final –e and common vowel team conventions for representing long vowel sounds. d. Use knowledge that every syllable must have a vowel sound to determine the number of syllables in a printed word. e. Decode two-syllable words following basic patterns by breaking the words into syllables. f. Read words with inflectional endings. g. Recognize and read grade-appropriate irregularly spelled words.

Reading Standards: Foundational Skills K-5 (FS – cont.)

FS		Grade 2 Students	Grade 3 Students
	Phonics and Word Recognition #3	**FS.2.3** Know and apply grade-level phonics and word analysis skills in decoding words. a. Distinguish long and short vowels when reading regularly spelled one-syllable words. b. Know spelling-sound correspondences for additional common vowel teams. c. Decode regularly spelled two-syllable words with long vowels. d. Decode words with common prefixes and suffixes. e. Identify words with inconsistent but common spelling-sound correspondences. f. Recognize and read grade-appropriate irregularly spelled words.	**FS.3.3** Know and apply grade-level phonics and word analysis skills in decoding words. a. Identify and know the meaning of the most common prefixes and derivational suffixes. b. Decode words with common Latin suffixes. c. Decode multisyllable words. d. Read grade-appropriate irregularly spelled words.

Reading Standards: Foundational Skills K-5 (FS – cont.)

FS		Kindergarten Students	Grade 1 Students	Grade 2 Students	Grade 3 Students
	Fluency #4	**RI.K.4** Read emergent-reader texts with purpose and understanding.	**RI.1.4** Read with sufficient accuracy and fluency to support comprehension. a. read on-level text with purpose and understanding. b. Read on-level text orally with accuracy, appropriate rate, and expression on successive readings. c. Use context to confirm or self-correct word recognition and understanding, rereading as necessary.	**RI.2.4** Read with sufficient accuracy and fluency to support comprehension. a. Read on-level text with purpose and understanding. b. Read on-level text orally with accuracy, appropriate rate, and expression on successive readings. c. Use context to confirm or self-correct word recognition and understanding, rereading as necessary.	**RI.3.4** Read with sufficient accuracy and fluency to support comprehension. a. Read on-level text with purpose and understanding. b. Read on-level prose and poetry orally with accuracy, appropriate rate, and expression on successive readings. c. Use context to confirm or self-correct word recognition and understanding, rereading as necessary.

Speaking and Listening Standards K-5 (SL)

*Sample of two standards relating to Reading.

Source: Common Core State Standards Initiative

www.corestandards.org/the-standards/english-language-arts-standards

SL	Anchor Standards for Speaking and Listening	Kindergarten Students	Grade 1 Students	Grade 2 Students	Grade 3 Students
Comprehension and Collaboration	Prepare for and participate effectively in a range of conversations and collaborations with diverse partners, building on others' ideas and expressing their own clearly and persuasively.	SL.K.1b 1. Participate in collaborative conversations with diverse partners about *kindergarten topics and texts* with peers and adults in small and larger groups. b) Continue a conversation through multiple exchanges.	SL.1.1b 1. Participate in collaborative conversations with diverse partners about *grade 1 topics and texts* with peers and adults in small and larger groups. b) Build on others' talk in conversations by responding to the comments of others through multiple exchanges.	SL.2.1b 1. Participate in collaborative conversations with diverse partners about *grade 2 topics and texts* with peers and adults in small and larger groups. b) Build on others' talk in conversations by linking their comments to the remarks of others.	SL.3.1b 1. Engage effectively in a range of collaborative discussions (one-on-one, in groups, and teacher-led) with diverse partners on *grade 3 topics and texts*, building on others' ideas and expressing their own clearly. b) Follow agreed-upon rules for discussions (e.g., gaining the floor in respectful ways, listening to others with care, speaking one at a time about the topics and texts under discussion).
Presentation of Knowledge and Ideas	Present information, findings, and supporting evidence such that listeners can follow the line of reasoning and the organization, development, and style are appropriate to task, purpose, and audience.	SL.K.4 Describe familiar people, places, things, and events and, with prompting and support, provide additional detail.	SL.1.4 Describe people, places, things, and event with relevant details, expressing ideas and feelings clearly.	SL.2.4 Tell a story or recount an experience with appropriate facts and relevant, descriptive details, speaking audibly in coherent sentences.	SL.3.4 Report on a topic or text, tell a story, or recount an experience with appropriate facts and relevant, descriptive details, speaking clearly at an understandable pace.

Denise M. Gudwin, Ph.D. Appendix

Language Standards K-5 (L) * Sample of two standards relating to Reading
Source: Common Core State Standards Initiative
www.corestandards.org/the-standards/english-language-arts-standards

L	Anchor Standards for Language	Kindergarten Students	Grade 1 Students	Grade 2 Students	Grade 3 Students
Vocabulary Acquisition and Use	Demonstrate understanding of figurative language, word relations, and nuances in word meanings.	**L.K.5a and L.K.5d** With guidance and support from adults, explore word relationships and nuances in word meanings. a) Sort common objects into categories (e.g., shapes, foods) to gain a sense of the concepts the categories represent. d) Distinguish shades of meaning among verbs describing the same general action (e.g., *walk, march, strut, prance*) by acting out the meanings.	**L.1.5a and L.1.5d** With guidance and support from adults, demonstrate understanding of word relationships and nuances in word meanings. a) Sort words into categories (e.g., colors, clothing) to gain a sense of the concepts the categories represent. d) Distinguish shades of meaning among verbs differing in manner (e.g., *look, peek, glance, stare, glare, scowl*) and adjectives differing in intensity (e.g., *large, gigantic*) by defining or choosing them or by acting out the meanings.	**L.2.5a and L.2.5b** Demonstrate understanding of word relationships and nuances in word meanings. a) Identify real-life connections between words and their use (e.g., describe foods that are *spicy or juicy*). b) Distinguish shades of meaning among closely related verbs (e.g., *toss, throw, hurl*) and closely related adjectives (e.g., *thin, slender, skinny, scrawny*).	**L.3.5a and L.3.5c** Demonstrate understanding of word relationships and nuances in word meanings. a) Distinguish the literal and nonliteral meanings of words and phrases in context (e.g., *take steps*). c) Distinguish shades of meaning among related words that describe states of mind or degrees of certainty (e.g. *knew, believed, suspected, heard, wondered*).

© Gudwin, D. www.denise.gudwin.org

COMMON CORE STANDARDS CITED IN RESOURCE HANDBOOK

Reading Standards for Literature (RL)

	RL.-.1	RL.-.2	RL.-.3	RL.-.4	RL.-.5	RL.-.6	RL.-.7	RL.-.8	RL.K.9	RL.-.10
Kindergarten	X	X	X		X	X			X	
1st Grade		X					X			
2nd Grade		X	X	X		X	X			

* Plus 3rd grade sample – RL.3.6

Reading Standards for Informational Text (RI)

	RI.-.1	RI.-.2	RI.-.3	RI.-.4	RI.-.5	RI.-.6	RI.-.7	RI.-.8	RI.-.9	RI.-.10
Kindergarten					X	X				
1st Grade					X	X				
2nd Grade	X		X		X	X	X			

Reading Standards: Foundational Skills (FS)

	RF.-.1	FR.-2	RF.-.3	RF.-.4
Kindergarten	X (a) X (b) X (c) X (d)		X (a)	
1st Grade				
2nd Grade				

Speaking and Listening Standards

	SL.-.1	SL.-2	SL.-3	SL.-.4	SL.-.5	SL.-.6
Kindergarten	X X (a)					
1st Grade						
2nd Grade	X X (b)	X		X	X	X

Language Standards (L)

	L.-.1	L.-.2	L.-.3	L.-.4	L.-.5
Kindergarten	X (a) X (b) X (c)	X X (a)			X (b)
1st Grade					
2nd Grade		X X (b)		X X (d) X (e)	X X (b)

Writing

	W.-.1	W.-.2	W.-.3	W.-.4	W.-5	W.-.6	W.-.7	W.-8
Kindergarten	X	X	X		X		X	X
1st Grade								
2nd Grade		X			X	X		

Sample Mentor Texts with Author, Illustrator, Levels, and Description

In an effort to provide you with more information on the mentor texts referred to through Common Core, I retrieved the following information from Scholastic.com (Book Wizard), Amazon.com, Barnesandnoble.com, and Lexile.com:

Personal Narrative

Title, Author and Illustrator, Genre	Description	Levels
A Chair for My Mother Vera B. Williams Illustrated by Caroline Binch Genre/Theme: Realistic Fiction	After a fire destroys their home and possessions, Rosa, her mother, and grandmother save and save until they can afford to buy one big, comfortable chair that all three of them can enjoy. "A superbly conceived picture book expressing the joyful spirit of a loving family." Horn Book	Interest Level: K – 2 Grade Level Equivalent: 3.3 Lexile ®: 640L DRA: 24 Guided Reading: M
When I Was Young in the Mountains Cynthia Rylant Illustrated by Diane Goode Genre/Theme: Realistic Fiction	"An evocative remembrance of the simple pleasures in county living; splashing in the swimming hole, taking baths in the kitchen, sharing family times, each is eloquently portrayed here in both the misty-hued scenes and in the poetic text." Association for Childhood Education International.	Interest Level: K – 2 Grade Level Equivalent: 3.7 Lexile ®: AD980L (Intended to be read aloud to a child rather than for the child to read it for the first time independently)

Narrative Stories

Title, Author and Illustrator, Genre	Description	Levels
The Recess Queen Alexis O'Neil, Illustrated by Laura Huliska-Beith Genre/Theme: Realistic Fiction	A fresh and original twist on the common issue of bullying. Kids will relate, and parents and teachers will appreciate the story's deft handling of conflict resolution, which happens without adult intervention.	Interest Level: Pre-K – 3 Grade Level Equivalent: 2.6 Lexile ®: 450L
Amazing Grace Mary Hoffman Illustrated by Caroline Binch Genre/Theme: Realistic Fiction	Grace loves stories, whether they're from books, movies, or the kind her grandmother tells. So when she gets a chance to play a part in Peter Pan, she knows exactly who she wants to be. Remarkable watercolor illustrations give full expression to Grace's high-flying imagination.	Interest Level: Gr 1 – 3 Grade Level Equivalent: 4.1 Lexile ®: AD980L (Adult Directed – Intended to be read aloud to a child rather than for the child to read it for the first time independently)

Realistic Fiction

Title, Author and Illustrator, Genre	Description	Levels
The Night Tree Eve Bunting Illustrated by Ted Rand Genre/Theme: General Fiction	By moonlight in the quiet forest, a young boy and his family decorate their favorite tree with popcorn, apples, tangerines, and sunflower-seed balls as a gift to the animals of the woods. "Sure to become a Christmas favorite, this beautifully illustrated story of a family's unusual tradition brings to life the true spirit of Christmas." American Bookseller	Interest Level: K – 2 Grade Level Equivalent: 2.8 Lexile ®: 620L DRA: 24 Guided Reading: K
My Rotten Red Headed Older Brother Patricia Polacco Genre/Theme: General Fiction	There's nothing worse than a rotten red-headed older brother! Patricia's brother Richard can run the fastest, climb the highest, spit the farthest, and still smile his extra-rotten, greeny-toothed, wasel-eyed grin. But when little Patricia wishes on a shooting star that she could do something – anything – to show him up, she finds out just what wishes – and older rotten redheaded older brothers – can really do. A lively and warmhearted tale of comic one-upmanship and brotherly love.	Interest Level: Gr 3 – 5 Grade Level Equivalent: 3.9 Lexile ®: 480L DRA: 28 Guided Reading: M

Functional Letters

Title, Author and Illustrator, Genre	Description	Levels
Dear Mrs. LaRue Mark Teague Genre/Theme: Comedy and Humor, Mystery and Suspense/ Personal and Persuasive Letter Writing	Through a series of hilarious letters home, Ike tries everything to get released from obedience school. Not until the madcap climax – involving a daring rescue with tricks learned at school – does Ike work his way back into Mrs. LaRue's good graces and move back home… Mrs. LaRue is Mark's most fetching book to date.	Interest Level: K – 3 Grade Level Equivalent: 3.1 Lexile ®: 500L
I Wanna Iguana Karen Kaufman Orloff Illustrated by David Catrow Genre/Theme: Comedy and Humor, Animal Stories	Alex just has to convince his mom to let him have an iguana, so he puts his arguments in writing. He promises that she won't have to feed it or clean its cage or even see it if she doesn't want to. Of course Mom imagines life with a six-foot-long iguana eating them out of house and home… This will have kids in hysterics as the negotiations go back and forth through notes.	Interest Level: K – 2 Grade Level Equivalent: 2.3 Lexile ®: AD460L (Adult Directed – Intended to be read aloud to a child rather than for the child to read it for the first time independently) DRA: 18-20 Guided Reading: J

Expository: How To/Recipe

Title, Author and Illustrator, Genre	Description	Levels
How to Lose All Your Friends Nancy Carlson Illustrated by Genre/Theme: General Fiction	This book offers advice on the kinds of things to do if you don't want any friends. With exuberant pictures and tongue-in-check sense of humor, the author takes a light-hearted look at bratty behavior that will have children laughing in recognition while learning exactly how not to behave.	Interest Level: K – 2 Grade Level Equivalent: 2.5 Lexile ®: 480L DRA: 16 Guided Reading: I School Library Journal lists it from PreK-1
Pancakes for Breakfast Tomie dePaola Genre/Theme: Comedy and Humor, How To, Wordless P	A wordless picture book follows the trials a little old lady who attempts to make pancakes for her breakfast. "The optimistic determination of the woman and the gentle humor of the illustrations make this an appealing book for the very young." School Library Journal	Interest Level: Pre-K – 1 Grade Level Equivalent: 1.1 Lexile ®: NP

LET'S WALK THROUGH ANOTHER STANDARD...

	Kindergartners:	**Grade 1 Students**	**Grade 2 Students**
Key Ideas & Details #2 Determine central ideas or themes of a text & analyze their development; summarize the key supporting details & ideas.	**With prompting & support,** retell **f**amiliar stories, including key details	Retell stories, including key details, & **demonstrate understanding of their central message or lesson**	Recount stories, including **fables & folktales from diverse cultures** & determine their central message, lesson, or moral
	Where are our students going? **Grade 3**: Recount stories, including fables, folktales, **& myths** from diverse cultures; determine the central message, lesson, or moral **& explain how it is conveyed through key details in the text.** **Grade 4 & 5**: Determine **a theme**…		

SELF-REFLECTION QUESTIONS

	Yes	No	I Need
I am comfortable with my previous State Standards.			
I am able to adapt lessons.			
I work collaboratively with numerous personnel for the sake of my students.			
I am competent and confident in gathering information about the Common Core.			
I am willing to find a way to be successful with the change in Standards.			
I feel comfortable with the Common Core Standards for my grade level.			
I still have questions about the Common Core Standards.			
I meet consistently and regularly with my grade group.			
My administrator is supportive in our efforts.			
I have implemented an efficient way to manage it all in my classroom.			
I feel comfortable gathering information online and on my own.			
I have the support I need from my colleagues.			
I have someone I can go to for help with the Common Core Standards.			

Teachers _____

Week Of _____

Independent Work Management Chart

Students	Monday	Tuesday	Wednesday	Thursday	Friday

USING ASSESSMENT RESULTS: MONITORING AND GROUPING, BASED ON STUDENT DATA

- ❏ PHONEMIC AWARENESS
- ❏ VOCABULARY
- ❏ COMPREHENSION
- ❏ OTHER _____
- ❏ PHONICS
- ❏ FLUENCY
- ❏ BACKGROUND KNOWLEDGE

NOTE: STUDENTS ARE GROUPED FOR FLUID (CHANGING) SMALL GROUP INSTRUCTION FOR MINI-LESSONS TO SUPPORT THE ACHIEVEMENT OF THE STANDARDS OR SKILLS LISTED BELOW.

	HIGH RISK (Names of Students)	MEDIUM RISK (Names of Students)	LOW RISK (Names of Students)
STANDARD OR SKILL:			
STANDARD OR SKILL:			
STANDARD OR SKILL:			
STANDARD OR SKILL:			

PHONICS
Learning the following 37 basic rimes (spelling patterns) assist children in reading and spelling over 500 primary level words.
Cunningham (2000)

ack	all	ain	ail	ale	ame
an	ank	ap	ash	at	ate
aw	ay	eat	ell	est	ice
ick	ide	ight	ill	in	ine
ing	ink	ip	it	ock	oke
op	ore	ot	uck	ug	ump
unk					

Phonics Elements
According to P. Cunningham (2000, p. 5), the following order is recommended when teaching phonics:

Most Useful Consonants:
b c d f g h j k l m n p r s t w

Short Vowel Patterns:
a (as in at); e (as in end); I (as in it); o (as in on); u (as in up)

Digraphs:
ch sh th ck

Long Vowel Patterns:
o (no); e (he); i-e (ride); igh (night); o-e (those); u-e (use); ay (day); ai (rain); ee (see); ea (eat); oa (float)

R-Controlled Vowels:
ar (car); or (for); er (her); ir (girl); ur (hurt)

Other Common Vowel Patterns:
oi (oil); oy (boy); aw (saw); au (because); al (walk); ou (cloud); ow (now and slow); oo (zoo and look); ew (new); y (my and very)

Blends:
bl br cl cr dr fl fr gl gr pl pr sc sk sl sm sn st sw tr

Endings:
s; ed; ing; er (person); er (more); est (most) ly

THE FLUENCY CHUNK

Sample: Slugs and Snails, Informational Text

By Claire Llewellyn and Barrie Watts

What Are Slugs and Snails? (pg. 6)

Slugs and snails belong to a large family of animals called mollusks.

A mollusk is a creature with a soft, slimy body, which is often protected by a shell.

Slugs and snails are very alike. The big difference between them is that snails have shells and slugs do not.

Possible Target Words:

| slugs | snails | creature |

| protected | slimy | shell |

Use Student Fluency Norms For Measuring Fluency Rate

FLUENCY RATES – WORDS CORRECT PER MINUTE

According to Dr. Timothy Rasinski (2003, p. 170), the following table provides the typical reading rates (wcpm = words correct per minute) for students. Doing a one-minute probe can provide you with valuable information if repeated and tracked over time, and will help you develop instruction for that particular student, focusing on his/her fluency needs.

Grade	Fall	Winter	Spring
1	--	--	60 wcpm
2	53	78	94
3	79	93	114
4	99	112	118
5	105	118	128
6	115	132	145

Sample of Fluency Probe

www.interventioncentral.org.

Intervention Central. Resource for Chart Dog and OKAPI! The Internet Application for Creating Curriculum-Based Assessment Reading Probe and much more.

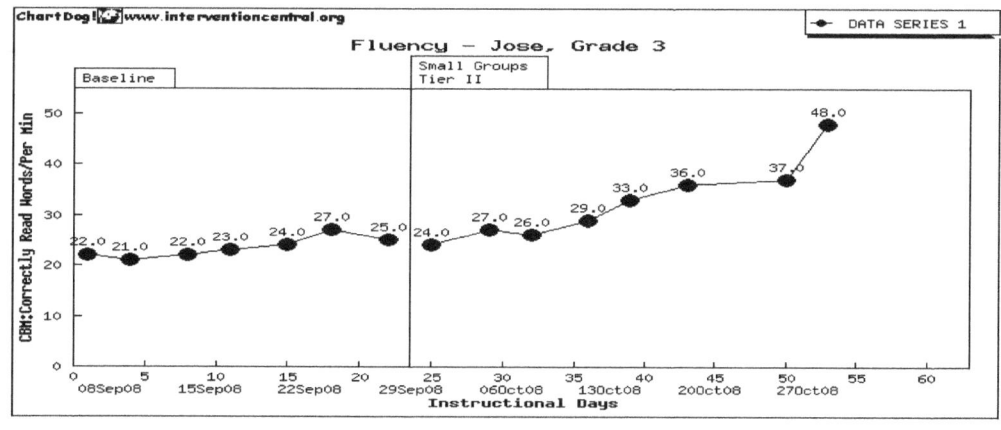

© Gudwin, D. www.denise.gudwin.org

QUICK FLUENCY CHECK

Teacher _____   Intervention Group _____

Text or Book _____, Level _____

Notes:	Student _____ Date Assessed _____	Student _____ Date Assessed _____	Student _____ Date Assessed _____	Student _____ Date Assessed _____
Word-by-word reading				
Phrase reading				
Sentence reading				
Appropriate expression used				
Tone of voice is relaxed				
The "flow" of the sentence is smooth.				
Student is aware of fluency rate (as indicated by charting or reviewing with teacher)				
Connections are made to reading (text-to-self, text-to-text, text-to-world)				

Learning Log

Title and Author	Predictions (Beginning)	Predictions (During)
_____	_____	_____

Main Characters	Reread Sections	Highlighted, underlined, or written margin notes
_____	❏ yes, p. _____ _____ ❏ no	❏ yes, p. _____ ❏ no

Other Strategies I used:	10 Finger Summary	Problems and Solutions
_____	_____	_____

Recommendation Rating to a Friend…

1 2 3 4 5 6 7 8 9 10

_____

4-Point Story Board: Sample of Possible "Assignments" Using a Story Board

Visualize the beginning of the story. Write or draw the picture in your mind.	Find three (3) action words in the story. Write them below and draw a picture of each. _____ _____ _____
Write a question you wish your teacher would ask you about this book. _____ _____ Then write the answer! _____ _____ _____	Retell the story. You may do it by writing it, telling it to your partner, or drawing a picture. _____ I will write it. _____ I will retell it to _____ _____ I will draw it.

6-Point Story Board: Sample of Possible "Assignments" Using a Story Board

Make a prediction of the story, based on the front cover.	Find five (5) verbs in the story. Write them below, add a synonym, for each. (Bonus: highlight the sentence where you found the verb.)	Were you able to make a connection to the character, setting, or story? Describe your connection.
Change the ending of the story.	If you were the main character, what would you do differently?	How did the main character change from the beginning of the story to the end?

© Gudwin, D. www.denise.gudwin.org

Two-Column Notes (T-Chart)

Choices (This can be the beginning of an Anchor Chart☺

- Vocabulary ---------------------------- Meaning
- Main Idea ----------------------------- Details
- Fact ----------------------------------- Opinion
- Author states ------------------------- I would say
- Target word --------------------------- Page it's on
- Supporting Details -------------------- Important Words
- Humor --------------------------------- Sentence in Context
- Author's Point of View --------------- My Perception
- Cause ---------------------------------- Effect
- Problem ------------------------------- Solution
- Compare ------------------------------ Contrast
- Prediction ---------------------------- What Happened
- Character ----------------------------- Description
- Opinion ------------------------------- Support for Opinion
- Situations ---------------------------- Consequences
- Telling Sentence (Writing) ---------- Showing Sentence

Venn Diagrams (Comparison Maps)

| Comparing Sample 1 to Sample 2 |

| Differences | | Differences |

| Similarities |

Conclusion

(Organize your thoughts in writing … Summarize, Compare and Contrast)

_____
_____
_____
_____
_____
_____
_____
_____
_____

Use Hula Hoops as a Venn Diagram, as discussed at the seminar.

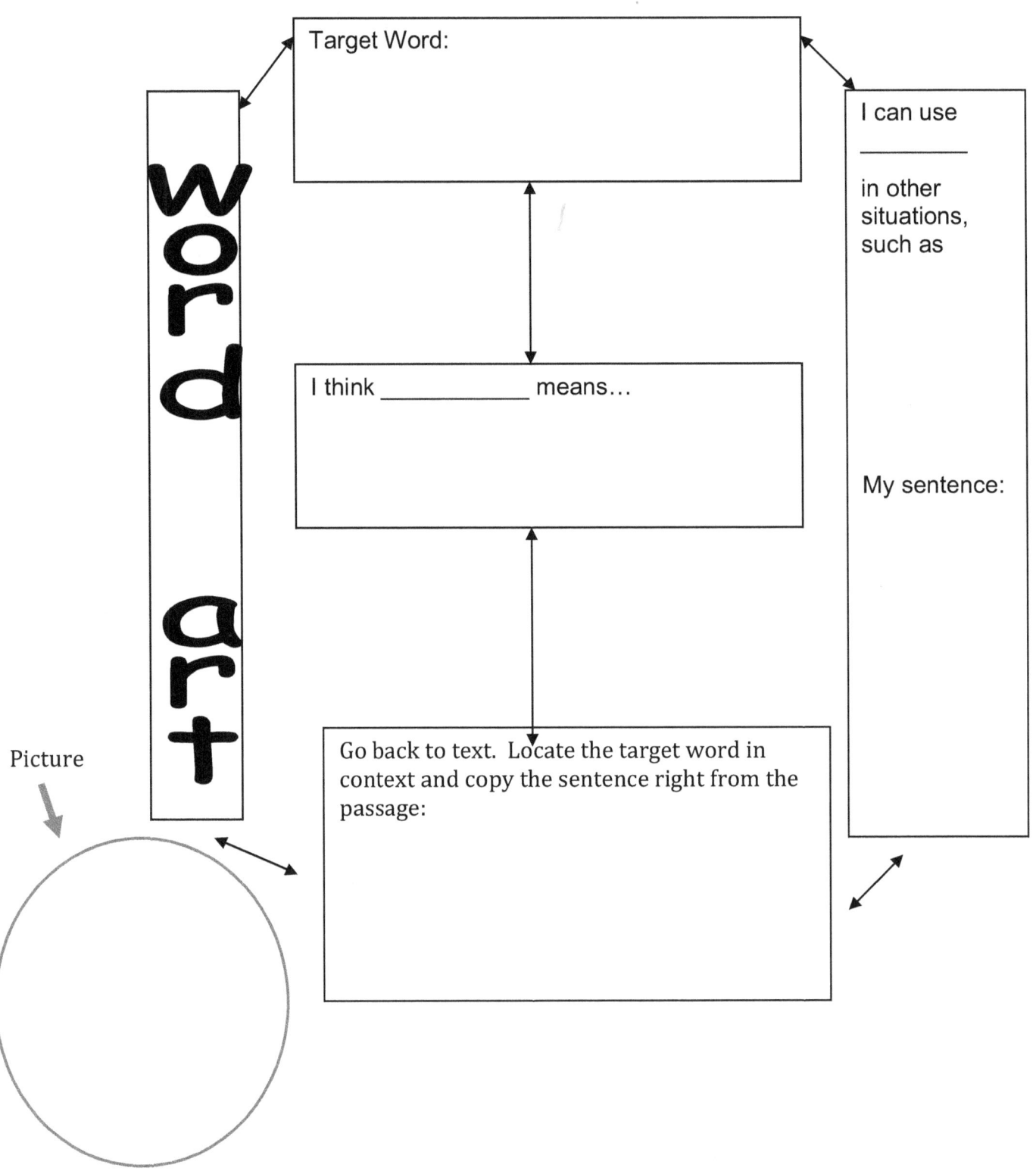

My Weekly Collection of Words, Words, Words

(Adapted from Janet Allen, 2000)

Words that give me goosebumps:	Words that are silly and make me laugh:	Words that I can visualize in my mind easily:
1. _____ 2. _____ 3. _____ 4. _____ 5. _____ 6. _____	1. _____ 2. _____ 3. _____ 4. _____ 5. _____ 6. _____	1. _____ 2. _____ 3. _____ 4. _____ 5. _____ 6. _____
Words that make noises:	**Words that show action:**	**Words that describe:**
1. _____ 2. _____ 3. _____ 4. _____ 5. _____ 6. _____	1. _____ 2. _____ 3. _____ 4. _____ 5. _____ 6. _____	1. _____ 2. _____ 3. _____ 4. _____ 5. _____ 6. _____
Weird words:	**Words that make me want to cry:**	**Words that my friends/family don't know:**
1. _____ 2. _____ 3. _____ 4. _____ 5. _____ 6. _____	1. _____ 2. _____ 3. _____ 4. _____ 5. _____ 6. _____	1. _____ 2. _____ 3. _____ 4. _____ 5. _____ 6. _____

© Gudwin, D. www.denise.gudwin.org

Name _____
Date _____

Character Analysis

What do I know about my characters?

Title of Book/Passage: _____

	Character # 1 _____ Name	Character # 2 _____ Name	Character # 3 _____ Name
What is his/her point of view?			
What do you think would be his/her favorite food to eat?			
What is he/she good at?			
What is he/she not so good at?			
What does he/she say?			
What does he/she look like?			
What bothers him/her the most?			
How would you change him/her?			
What do friends and family think?			

QARs Question-Answer Relationship – Purpose…Feedback…Support

In the Book
The answer is right there, in the text.

In My Head
Author and You…The answer is not in the story. Think about what you already know with what the author

Think and Search, Put it all Together
You have to put information together from different parts of the reading

On My Own
The answer is not in the reading selection. Use your own experiences, your prior knowledge.

Responding to Literature

I wonder why…

I liked it when…

I noticed that…

I was surprised when…

I know the feeling…

If I were….

I discovered…

I loved the way…

I remember…

This reminds me of…

It made me smile when…

It scared me when…

A question that I have…

Miami-Dade County Public Schools, Division of Language Arts/Reading

Retelling Log

Title and Author	Buddy and Pair-Share Reflection
_____	_____
_____	_____
_____	_____

Borrowed Bits	Highlights of my Final Revision
_____	_____
_____	_____
Muddled Meanings	_____
_____	_____
	_____
	_____

Linguistic Spillover Used	My favorite word or phrase used by the author:
_____	_____
_____	_____
_____	_____
_____	_____
_____	_____
_____	
	Connection to something I know, something I've experienced:
	_____
	_____
	_____
	_____
	_____

THINK ALOUDS = CONVERSATIONS

✓   If you completed it with your buddy (Pair-Share)

\-   If you did not

Situation	Think Aloud	Expand on it	Reflect
How to make a peanut butter and jelly sandwich.	✓	✓	-

ACCOMMODATIONS CHECKLIST FOR A LITTLE EXTRA HELP

Adapted from Beech, M. (1999). *Accommodations: Assisting Students with Disabilities. A Guide for Educators.*

Instructional Methods and Materials

Student has difficulty identifying main ideas or important points
- ☑ Highlight important points of the text to draw attention. Tell the student to read these points first.
- ☑ Give the student a list of important vocabulary ahead of time.
- ☑ Have the student read the summary or objectives first.
- ☑ Have the student read the review questions first, then look for the answers.
- ☑ Give the student a worksheet or study guide to follow when doing independent reading.
- ☑ Use hands-on activities, pictures, or diagrams to provide alternate ways of learning abstract concepts or complex information.
- ☑ Let the student use sticky notes or an erasable highlighter to mark key points in the textbook.
- ☑ Let the student use a book written at a lower grade level. This can let the student pay more attention to the main ideas.

Student can understand the information, but has difficulty reading the required materials
- ☑ Provide an audio version of the material. Use books-on-tape or have an assistant, volunteer, or other student make a recording.
- ☑ Provide alternate materials with similar content at a lower reading level.
- ☑ Use a videotape or movie that presents the same information.
- ☑ Use assistive technology to transfer printed words to speech.
- ☑ Have a learning buddy read aloud textbooks or other printed material.

Student has difficulty with most lessons

Student needs help to get ready for the lesson
- ☑ Introduce new vocabulary prior to lesson; use visual aids (chalkboard, overhead, charts).
- ☑ Use advance organizers to alert students to what will be included & expected from the lesson.
- ☑ Provide an overview of the content or expected learning at the beginning of the session.

Student needs help during the lesson
- ☑ Preset material in a logical manner & use explicit cues to shift from one aspect to the next.
- ☑ Promote active involvement of students by asking questions or breaking up the lecture with small group interaction, discussion, or structured responses.
- ☑ Break the information into steps or key components & monitor the student's comprehension as it is presented.
- ☑ Provide oral & visual clues during discussion about what is important to include in notes. Write important ideas on the board or chart paper. Use different color chalk or markers for emphasis
- ☑ Provide structured organizers for note taking, such as a copy of overheads, outline or graphic organizers.
- ☑ Use NCR, carbon paper, or photocopying for peers to take notes that can be shared.
- ☑ Teach the student how to use a two-column note taking format or concept mapping for notes.
- ☑ Key class notes to the relevant pages in textbook.
- ☑ Let the student record class lectures & discussions.

Student needs help after the lesson
- ☑ Repeat, paraphrase, & summarize all important points, at the conclusion of the discussion.
- ☑ Ask the student to paraphrase key points in his/her own words & identify anything that is unclear.
- ☑ Prepare a summary of important information
- ☑ Use cooperative learning techniques such as Think-Pair-Share or Jigsaw to have the students review key points.
- ☑ Ask the student to tell or write the important information that was included in the lesson before the class ends. Encourage the student to ask questions.
- ☑ Arrange for time to meet with the student after class to clarify any questions.

Student has difficulty with Assignments

Student has difficulty following instructions
- ☑ *Student needs help to <u>get ready</u> for the instructions.*
- ☑ Use a prearranged signal to gain attention before giving directions.
- ☑ Make sure the student is facing you when instructions are given.
- ☑ Change your tone of voice to alert the student & sustain attention.
- ☑ Give the student an agenda or schedule for each day.

Student needs help <u>while</u> you are giving instructions
- ☑ Combine oral directions with pictures, words, or diagrams.
- ☑ Read written directions orally before students start the assignment.
- ☑ When modeling expected behavior, describe critical components.
- ☑ Complete sample problems or tasks to show the student what is expected.
- ☑ Have the student paraphrase instructions or show you what to do.
- ☑ Repeat & simplify instructions for the student.
- ☑ Give the student a description of expected behaviors or the rubric to be used for evaluation.
- ☑ Give step-by-step instructions for an activity with the steps outlined in writing or shown in picture sequences.

Student needs help <u>after</u> the instructions
- ☑ Assign a study buddy to help the student when needed.
- ☑ Check to see if the student needs any assistance in getting started.

Student has difficulty completing assignments
- ☑ Break long-term assignments into sections with corresponding due dates.
- ☑ Teach the student to maintain a calendar of assignments.
- ☑ Give the student an individual responsibility checklist.
- ☑ Give the student a choice of tasks & assignments.
- ☑ Have the student keep a journal or homework log that includes the directions & timelines.
- ☑ Communicate homework assignments & expectations to parents so they can help, if needed.
- ☑ At first, give partial credit for late assignments or incomplete work until the student is able to complete the work on time.

Student gets confused by complex materials
- ☑ Indicate sections on paper for each response by drawing lines or folding.
- ☑ Use different kinds of paper for different assignments, such as graph paper notes.
- ☑ Use color-coding to help students identify tasks, meanings, or expectations.
- ☑ Show students how to cover parts of text or worksheet not being used.
- ☑ Give page numbers for locating answers to questions in textbook.
- ☑ Simplify directions by numbering each step.

Student needs help organizing or keeping track of materials
- ☑ Let the student use a special folder or binder to keep materials organized. Use dividers or folders to keep subjects organized & use color-coding by unit or subject.
- ☑ Give the student a compartmentalized container for classroom materials, tools, & supplies.
- ☑ Let the student use physical supports such as bookends, plastic containers to keep supplies, or bags or folders for work materials.
- ☑ Place a timetable or assignment list on the student's desk.

REFLECTIVE NOTE PAGE

❑ To Do... ❑ Notes: Topic _____

REFLECTIVE NOTE PAGE

❏ To Do...   ❏ Notes: Topic _____

ONGOING TO-DO LIST

Add to your list as you hear of great ideas – they will be all on one page!

What students read may now be as important as **how** they read. What's **NEW**?

Supplemental Information for Appendix A,

Figure 1 [Revised] Updated Text Complexity Grade Bands and Associated Ranges from Multiple Measures

Common Core Band	ATOS	Degrees of Reading Power ®	Flesch-Kincaid	The Lexile Framework ®	Reading maturity	Source-Rater
2nd-3rd	2.75-5.14	42-54	1.98-5.34	420-820	3.53-6.13	0.05-2.48
4th-5th	4.97-7.03	52-60	4.51-7.73	740-1010	5.42-7.92	0.84-5.75
6th-8th	7.00-9.98	57-67	6.51-10.34	925-1185	7.04-9.57	4.11-10.66
9th-10th	9.67-12.01	62-72	8.32-12.12	1050-1335	8.41-10.81	9.02-13.93
11th-CCR	11.20-14.10	67-74	10.34-14.2	1185-1385	9.57-12.00	12.30-14.50

This more recent chart gives a more flexible ascending band, especially in the lower grades. Suggestion: Use more than one measure.

- Atos by Renaissance Learning
- Degrees of Reading Power ® (DRPA ®) by Questar Assessment, Inc
- Flesch-Kincaid (public domain)
- The Lexile® Framework for Reading by MetaMetrics
- Reading Maturity by Pearson Education
- SourceRater by Educational Testing Service

The figure below is the original text complexity band from Appendix A (Figure 3) at www.corestandards.org.
NOTE: The last column is my added comparison

Text Complexity Grade Band in the Standards	Old Lexile ® Ranges	Recalibrated Lexile ® Ranges Aligned to CCR Expectations	REVISED Lexile Frame-work ® From above revised table
K-1	N/A	N/A	N/A
2-3	450-725	450-790	420-820
4-5	645-845	770-980	740-1010
6-8	860-1010	955-1155	925-1185
9-10	960-1115	1080-1305	1050-1335
11-CCR	1070-1220	1215-1355	1185-1385

© Gudwin, D. www.denise.gudwin.org

www.ingramcontent.com/pod-product-compliance
Lightning Source LLC
Chambersburg PA
CBHW081235170426
43198CB00017B/2765